Welcoming the Light of Christ

Also by Michael Perham and Kenneth Stevenson and published by SPCK:

WAITING FOR THE RISEN CHRIST
A Commentary on Lent, Holy Week, Easter: Services and Prayers

Welcoming the Light of Christ

Michael Perham and Kenneth Stevenson

Reference is sometimes made to the chapter numbers used in the report edition of *The Promise of His Glory*. Readers using the 1991 Mowbray/Church House Publishing edition should note the following changes:

p. 17, line 23, for 'Chapter 2' read 'Chapter 1'
p. 29, lines 10–11 up, should read, '. . . set out carefully in the Notes on "An Alternative Calendar" (see Appendix to *The Promise of His Glory*).'
p. 46, line 3, for 'Chapter 4' read 'Chapter 3'
p. 48, lines 6 and 20, for 'Chapter 2' read 'Chapter 1'
p. 50, line 22, for 'Chapter 4' read 'Chapter 3'
p. 61, line 7, for 'Chapter 5' read 'Chapter 4'
p. 69, line 5, for 'Chapter 2' read 'Chapter 1'
p. 101, line 17, for 'Lectionary B' read 'Lectionary 2'
p. 108, line 24, for 'chapter of' read 'Appendix to'

Michael Perham
and
Kenneth Stevenson

Welcoming the Light of Christ

A Commentary on
THE PROMISE OF HIS GLORY:
SERVICES AND PRAYERS FOR THE SEASON
FROM ALL SAINTS TO CANDLEMAS

First published in Great Britain 1991
SPCK
Holy Trinity Church
Marylebone Road
London NW1 4DU

British Library Cataloguing in Publication Data

Perham, Michael
Welcoming the Light of Christ
1. Christian life. Prayers - Devotional works
I. Title II. Stevenson, Kenneth
242.8

ISBN 0-281-04498-8

Printed in Great Britain by WBC Print Ltd, Bridgend

Contents

Preface vii

1 Introduction 1

2 The Service of Light 9

3 All Saintstide 21

4 Advent 38

5 Christmas 54

6 Epiphany 70

7 Candlemas 86

8 Lectionary 102

Select Bibliography 111

Preface

The Promise of His Glory is, we believe, one of the most exciting documents to emerge from the Church of England in our day. A companion to *Lent, Holy Week, Easter*, published in 1986, it is the work of the Church's Liturgical Commission and provides a rationale, together with services and resources, for the whole period from All Saints' Day to Candlemas, the Presentation of Christ in the Temple, that we hope will be found helpful not only to Anglicans, and not only in England. As members of the Commission that produced it, we have been glad to be part of a creative experience that has broken new ground for the Church's worship.

When *Lent, Holy Week, Easter* was published, we collaborated on the commentary to accompany it, published by SPCK under the title *Waiting for the Risen Christ*. We have now once again worked together on the commentary on *The Promise of His Glory*. Academic and pastoral concerns have been brought together, and the insights we have gained from working on the material for five years and using it experimentally have helped to shape what we hope will be a book that will encourage many to use *The Promise of His Glory* and to discover great riches in it.

We have not attempted to conflate our contributions, thus losing any individualism. Except in Chapter 1, which is entirely by Kenneth Stevenson, each chapter consists first of a section by Kenneth Stevenson, which in each case describes some of the background and history and sets the services within a broad context, and secondly a section by Michael Perham, which looks in detail at the services in the new book and how they might be used in ordinary congregations. There is overlap, of course, for theology, liturgy and pastoral considerations cannot and should not be kept apart.

Chapter 8 of this book is a little different from the others in that it anticipates the legalizing of material not yet authorized. In October 1990 the House of Bishops commended *The Promise of His Glory* in a form not much different from that in which it appeared as a report to synod earlier in the year.

Two important alterations were however made. One was the omission of new initiation material at Epiphany (see chapter 6), the other the removal to an appendix of the calendar, lectionary and collects. Unlike the rest of this book they have not yet been commended, and have to go through a process of synodical authorization. However this book was proceeded with on the assumption that they will be authorized, for without such authority the whole rationale of *The Promise of His Glory* falls away. We have therefore assumed the new calendar throughout the book, and written in chapter 8 about the lectionary in a way that anticipates its speedy approval along the lines proposed.

We are grateful to other members of the Liturgical Commission for their support, and particularly to David Stancliffe, the Provost of Portsmouth, who, as well as bearing a heavy responsibility in editing *The Promise*, has also made helpful suggestions for this commentary. We are grateful also to the people we serve in our parishes – Holy Trinity and St Mary's, Guildford and the Oakdale Team Ministry in Poole. Some of the material in *The Promise* was written originally for them, and much of it has been tried out on them. It has been their enthusiasm for it that has enabled us, in writing this commentary, to be confident that we are commending something the Church will find very good.

November 1990

Michael Perham
Kenneth Stevenson

ONE

Introduction

Hark the glad sound! the Saviour comes,
The Saviour promised long:
Let every heart prepare a throne,
And every voice a song.

He comes, the prisoners to release
In Satan's bondage held;
The gates of brass before him burst,
The iron fetters yield.

He comes, the broken heart to bind,
The bleeding soul to cure,
And with the treasures of his grace
To bless the humble poor.

Our glad Hosannas, Prince of Peace,
Thy welcome shall proclaim;
And heaven's eternal arches ring
With thy beloved name.

Philip Doddridge (1702–51), the author of that well-known hymn, was an unusual man, living at an unusual time. The first half of the eighteenth century was not a time of great religious fervour, nor was it known for its mutual religious tolerance. And yet from the heart of English Nonconformity there came a pastor and teacher, with an international reputation, who could combine strong religious conviction with a rare power over language at its most poetic. He states his case with economy, simplicity, directness. He is the same man who enthused about the importance of distributing Bibles to ordinary Christians, and he tried to heal some of the many wounds in English Dissent. (Of the eight ministers to take part in his ordination in 1730, five were Presbyterians.) But strangely, his hymns (which included 'Ye servants of the Lord', 'O God of Bethel', and 'My God, and is thy table spread') were only published posthumously. They quickly wormed their way into Anglican acceptance through the many hymn books of the following century.

But 'Hark the glad sound' was not written for Advent – and that is perhaps an important lesson as we begin to look at what some people regard as the heart of the 'winter season' of Christianity, from November to February. We, who are so used to time-locking the liturgical year and packaging God in the proper compartments, badly need to look afresh at the whole rationale for liturgical time. And the best way to start is to widen our concepts. Doddridge knew no such thing as the Church Year; it was unknown in eighteenth-century Nonconformity, since his own tradition had rejected the whole notion at the Reformation. Interestingly, the drift of liturgical renewal in our own century has seen the gradual absorption of a simplified Liturgical Year by nearly every branch of Protestantism. And that has meant bringing along many traditional resources (such as 'Hark the glad sound') and fitting them into this new framework.

But the hymn still stands on its own. Although most hymn books suggest its use in Advent, it is quite possible to sing it at other times. And that is really the underlying message of this book, and the services which it seeks to elucidate and reflect upon. If we are to be ready to celebrate 'The Promise of His Glory', then we have to be ready to see that in the Christian faith everything is connected to everything else. We do not move from one season to another in a mechanistic fashion. Rather, we move through one phase to another, mixing light and shade, feeling deeply here and rejoicing openly there. The Saviour who is promised long is ready to break through our religious conventions as well as our social behaviour. Philip Doddridge meant those words that Christ does indeed come to release those in bondage, and that includes those in religious bondage. The winter season of organized Christianity needs a dose of new life – and that is what *The Promise of His Glory* is trying to bring.

So why, then, this new set of services?

At one level, it has to be admitted that the previous publication, *Lent, Holy Week, Easter: Services and Prayers*, was received by the Church of England (and beyond) with greater enthusiasm than was anticipated. But the production of a companion volume has a far stronger rationale than that. For it is in the season leading up to Christmas that clergy and worship-leaders all over the country are hard-pressed to produce special services for all sorts of different groups. One of the features in the so-called 'decline of Christendom' is that many folk still want to come to church at festivals, but want to do this under the guise of a special organization.

The ramifications of this trend are much wider. It means that the whole pre-Christmas season (and it often feels like a season in its own right) is dominated by extras of one sort or another. On the one hand it is good for the Church to be faced with a 'consumer demand', but it places a strain on the traditional system, especially when that system seems to be worked out in a different way, placing the emphasis on a time of preparation, followed by a time of celebration, with accompanying minor feasts. *The Promise of His Glory* attempts to deal with an area of liturgical life that is not so easily identifiable as Lent, Holy Week and Easter, but which nonetheless figures prominently on many pastors' agendas. What, then, is the sweep of this book?

The Church's Year is centred on two basic cycles, those of Easter and Christmas. Each has a central core of celebration, for which the vestments are white, the hymns and music glorious, and the bible texts are full of rich stories that tell of the central acts of redemption. Each also has a period of extended celebration afterwards, in the course of which we should continue that celebration, so that the festival has its own season, and is not confined to one big day, after which it is all over. And each has a time of preparation, when more reflective moods prevail, the vestments are restrained in their colour, and the bible readings definitely lead up to and look forward to the central feast.

At Christmas, the way this works out, in theory at least, is that Christmas and Epiphany make up those central festivals, and that Advent is the time of preparation. Many churches which follow either the Prayer Book or the Alternative Service Book lectionary schemes will observe this approach, in slightly differing ways. But it has never been entirely satisfactory, and it fails to meet the ways in which religious observance has been shifting perceptibly over the past thirty years. Taking a leaf out of the ASB scheme, *The Promise of His Glory* wants to make much more of Advent, not as a clerical kill-joy, for the parson to frown through a purple stole at the thousandth school carol service, but rather as a season that has many rich resources in its tradition, both early and recent. It also wants to explore the riches of that tradition at Epiphany, which runs the risk of becoming something of a passenger, and a special liturgy for Epiphany-tide will be discussed later on, with its background.

But *The Promise of His Glory* also wants to extend this liturgical cycle in two other directions. First, the month of November is for many people a time of 'remembering' in many different ways. All Saints' Day has long been theoretically a major festival of the Church. Over the past century, All Souls' Day as a commemoration of the departed has come into people's spiritual diets, raising theological and pastoral issues, which we shall look at in due course. Remembrance Sunday is still an occasion when many churches are packed to the doors, and as the debate about war continues, and the average age of survivors from the two World Wars becomes ever greater, it is not infrequently a time of uncertainty in local congregations as to what to do. To be confronted by these religious observances within such a short space of time places on the Christian community an important opportunity to reflect carefully on what sanctification really means. Many people complain that public worship nowadays ignores the saints, and the reality of divine judgement. To gear the community up to dealing with these important realities, which people want to bring out, would seem to be a crucial prelude to Advent. All Saints' Day says that sanctity is accessible. All Souls' Day says that death is to be mourned – but in hope. Remembrance Sunday brings before the whole nation the full horror of war.

Then, *The Promise of His Glory*, in addition to emphasizing Epiphany, suggests that the Baptism of the Lord be observed as a Feast on the Sunday after. As will be seen, this enables the Church to bring into sharper focus the meaning of Christ's baptism, and this comes at an important time, because there is a fashion nowadays in preaching and liturgical texts to link baptism so strongly with Easter that we lose the opportunity of seeing how in the past it has been linked with other festivals, the most important being Epiphany itself.

Finally, the new services bring out the full implications of what is perhaps the most neglected festival in this cycle – Candlemas, the Presentation of Christ in the Temple. Long relegated to the margins, for the indulgence of the High Church, this day has one of the richest gospel texts of all, and a long and somewhat contradictory history. It also poses its own fundamental question, whether it should be the end of the Christmas cycle, or look forward, through its chilling message, to the ensuing Lent, Holy Week and Easter! Whatever the solution on paper to that problem, it is certainly the conviction of those who drafted *The Promise of His Glory* that Candlemas is no mere appendage, but comes as the conclusion of the whole Christmas season, and only after it should the vestments be changed from white to green.

It will be apparent by now that these services stand in direct relation to *Lent, Holy Week, Easter*. But, just to bring out the contrast further, there are some significant differences.

First of all, unlike the Easter cycle, where an exact 'chronology' is to a certain extent possible, and there is a long and generally accepted tradition of observance, this season is too mixed, ambiguous, and multi-faceted for the Church to be able to move exactly from one episode to another. (And in any case, as we have already said, that sort of approach is not desirable.) To take one example, at Christmas, there are only two Gospels (Matthew and Luke) which provide infancy narratives, but these are so different that it is damaging to the integrity of each to try to commemorate the 'events' (e.g. the flight into Egypt) at the supposedly 'exact' point.

Secondly, the sources for many of these services are very mixed. There has been no central core of special ceremonies, originating from Jerusalem and subsequently tamed by the West (e.g. Palm Processions), that has proved to have been of central inspiration. Indeed, the only two services that are of directly ancient background (apart from the Service of Light) are the Epiphany rite and Candlemas, but both these have been adapted. For those who think modern liturgy-drafters are antiquarians in disguise, this book may therefore come as a pleasant surprise!

Thirdly, while the Easter and Christmas cycles undergird the whole Church Year, the popularity of Christmas in commercial and family terms is a recent development. It may be that such popularity is spreading to Easter as well. But such a development places considerable apologetic demands on preaching and celebrating the Christmas message, with its surrounding infrastructure of Advent and Epiphany–Candlemas.

Fourthly, this popularity may be not unrelated to the pagan antecedents of northern Europe. My Viking ancestors ate and drank themselves into a stupor in order to celebrate the middle of winter! This sort of factor should not be ignored when we observe how the crazy consumerism surrounding the secular Christmas operates on people, whether they can afford the goods they are buying or not. But it may also explain the recurrence of the light–darkness theme through *The Promise of His Glory*. However mixed the culture may be of those individuals who will be using these services, their *context* is avowedly northern European, twentieth-century. Pagan archetypes have not completely disappeared.

Fifthly, the material in these services is more mixed than *Lent, Holy Week, Easter*, where there was a clear division between major services and supporting material. This means that there is a greater element of choice; more reliance is made on local churches to draw material together to suit their own circumstances.

Last and most important of all, unlike the Easter cycle, where a definite shape settles in fairly early on in all the main traditions of the East and West, this is not the case with the Advent–Candlemas sequence. Those who were brought up on the Prayer Book (with or without adaptations), and became accustomed to the ASB provisions, may be initially surprised at yet one more set of services. But as our discussion of the origins, development and meaning of each major item will show, history does not finally settle even such questions as the precise relationship between Christmas and Epiphany, let alone the length and significance of Advent, or (for that matter) the quasi-Wagnerian brooding that lies in the background to some of the hymns of the Byzantine rite for Candlemas. If the past is a bit of a mess, we must not expect neat and tidy solutions for today. Rather, we should almost expect people's needs, spiritual included, to change and develop as times goes on.

In our companion volume, *Waiting for the Risen Christ*, we drew attention to three pieties underlying the traditional observance of Lent, Holy Week and Easter. These were 'unitive', 'rememorative', and 'representational'. A 'unitive' piety undergirds the old Easter Vigil, celebrating death and resurrection in one single liturgy, before ever the rest of Holy Week was invented. A 'rememorative' piety is reflected in the Palm Procession, where the faithful carry a symbolic branch (no more) as they walk purposely from one place to another. A 'representational' piety comes across at its most obvious in the Stations of the Cross, where events are depicted directly, almost crudely.

Could a comparable way of looking at things be produced for Advent–Candlemas? There is no doubt that beneath many of the ancient observances of Christmas and Epiphany, 'unitive' piety, that celebrates the whole incarnation and not just the historic 'nativity', is to be found alive and kicking. 'Rememorative' rites persist in such simple expedients as the Service of Light, and the Epiphany liturgy, as well as the Candlemas services. 'Representational' piety rears its head in the more intimate customs, such as the baby in the crib, and the figures of the shepherds and the wise men. As with the services themselves, there is more of a mixture. But since that is the very nature of the material on offer in *The Promise of His Glory*, that should not surprise us.

If Philip Doddridge were here today, he would be amused at the new contexts in which his fine christological hymn is employed, whether at an Advent carol service, at a pre-Christmas Vigil, surrounded by candles, or at a Sunday morning Eucharist, with purple (or blue) vestments apparent. Among the many questions which he would ask of us would be what we understand by the nature of Christ's coming. *The Promise of His Glory*, if it does its job, will enable us to answer that question in many different ways. In a setting quite different from that of Doddridge, Nikolai Grundtvig wrote an Advent hymn in 1839 that begins, 'Be welcome, again, year of the Lord'. The first three verses look forward to Christmas, Easter and Pentecost, and the last offers the whole celebration to God's care, as the Church looks forward in joyful song to telling once more the wonders of the gospel.

TWO

The Service of Light

I

O joyous light of the holy glory of the immortal Father,
heavenly, holy, blessed Jesus Christ!
As we come to the setting of the sun and behold the
evening light,
We praise you Father, Son and Holy Spirit, God!
It is fitting at all times that you be praised with
auspicious voices, O Son of God, giver of life.
That is why the whole world glorifies you!

There are several versions of the ancient Greek hymn, *Phos hilaron*, and this is a literal version made by Robert Taft, one of the foremost scholars of Eastern Church worship today. This is how he describes the way in which it is used:

> . . . the priest and deacon, bearing the smoking censer, walk in procession through the church. On coming to the doors of the sanctuary, they intone the age-old Hymn of Light, the *Phos Hilaron*, which for over sixteen centuries, day after day, without variation or change, has proclaimed that the light of the world is not the sun of creation by day, nor the evening lamp by night, but the eternal Son of God, 'the true light that enlightens everyone', in the words of the prologue of St John's Gospel (1.9). I must confess that I find consolation in the company I am in when I intone this immortal hymn.
>
> (Robert F. Taft, *The Liturgy of the Hours in East and West: The Origins of the Divine Office and its Meaning for Today*, Collegeville, MN, Liturgical Press, 1986, p. 286)

The origins of this little hymn probably lie as far back as the third century. It was written to be used at daily evening prayer, when the lights were lit. For us who live in a quite different culture in which the mere move of a switch can light up artificially the most enormous spaces, it is hard to imagine – in one way – the real impact of this chant in the ancient world. And yet it is an irony that the sharing of light has grown in popularity all over the Western world today.

You will find candles frequently used at special services, as well as more regular ones. The 1985 Book of Alternative Services of the Anglican Church in Canada makes provision for the *Lucernare* (as it has been called in the Latin West) to precede Evening Prayer on any occasion, and also to lead into the Saturday Vigil of the Resurrection, whose history we shall look at shortly. It is this use that links most directly with the time-honoured custom of seeing every week as the embodiment of the whole Church Year, so that the Saturday Vigil commemorates the resurrection every week (as it does today at Taizé), looking forward to Sunday morning, and other days of the week develop their own special associations, such as the betrayal of Christ on Wednesdays and the crucifixion on Fridays.

But special ceremonies are no mere cute adjuncts to bald Christian worship, distractions for children while something more 'serious' is going on. The sharing of light at evening in Christian worship, as Taft makes plain, is a way of pointing to Christ as the one true light, that grants us the spiritual illumination that we need in order to make sense of the lives that we have to lead, in whatever context we find ourselves. And as with all really effective symbolism, there is an inherent ambiguity in what we are doing. Light at Christmas or Easter holds together birth and rebirth, in theological terminology, incarnation and atonement. It is not for nothing that *Phos hilaron* and its related customs grew up all over the ancient world. Basil of Caesarea, writing in the latter half of the fourth century, quotes it, and for him it was already ancient. He used it as proof of the early understanding in Christianity of the doctrine of the Trinity, because of its mention of Father, Son and Holy Spirit. It was clearly important for him to be able to go back in time to the era of the persecuted Church of the previous century (or even earlier?) in order to demonstrate the theological significance of worship, in which we are playing no mere game, but taking part in something infinitely mysterious and real.

It is fashionable these days to look for the origins of everything Christian in pagan backgrounds and often it is a helpful exercise. It usually shows that the Christian interpretation has struggled to articulate something important and crucial from a 'natural' background. For the early Christians to share light would have been obvious, particularly for those who had come from Judaism, where the lighting of lamps at the start of sabbaths (i.e. at Friday evening meal) was established custom. Interestingly, many of the first Christian communities took over this precise practice, and lit the lamps before their common meal (the 'agape'). At the start of the third century, in Rome, Hippolytus has this to say in his *Apostolic Tradition* about the procedure:

> When the bishop is present, and evening has come, a deacon brings in a lamp; and standing in the midst of all the faithful who are present [the bishop] shall give thanks. First he shall say this greeting: 'The Lord be with you.'
> And the people shall say: 'With your spirit.'
> [Bishop]: 'Let us give thanks to the Lord.'
> And they shall say: 'It is fitting and right: greatness and exaltation with glory are his due.'
> And he does not say, 'Up with your hearts', because that is said [only] at the offering [i.e. at the eucharistic prayer].
> And he shall pray thus, saying: 'We give you thanks, Lord, through your Son Jesus Christ our Lord, through whom you have shone upon us and revealed to us the inextinguishable light. So when we have completed the length of the day and have come to the beginning of the night, and have satisfied ourselves with the light of day which you created for our satisfying; and since now through your grace we do not lack the light of evening, we praise and glorify you through your Son Jesus Christ our Lord, through whom be glory and power and honour to you with the Holy Spirit, both now and always and to the ages of ages. Amen.'
> And all shall say 'Amen.'
> They shall rise, then, after supper and pray; and the boys and the virgins shall say psalms.
> (see Geoffrey J. Cuming, *Hippolytus: A Text for Students*, Grove Liturgical Study 8, Bramcote, Grove, 1976, pp. 23–4)

At the heart of this little rite are word and action in a perfect harmony. The one lamp is focused upon, while the bishop recites the prayer of thanksgiving, which sanctifies the time of day and places it overtly in the context of the eternal light of Christ. It is this kind of thanksgiving that forms the basis of many of the evening light-ceremonies that are to be found in modern service books, *The Promise of His Glory* included. But while the 'agape' persisted sporadically, evening services, whether of the 'vesper' or the 'vigil' type, developed too, and since they had to be conducted in the dark, it was inevitable that the *Lucernare* should also be used to introduce these as well. The origin of the Daily Prayer of the Church is a very complex subject and the early evidence can often be tantalizing. But, roughly speaking, there are three kinds of evening service that emerge in these early centuries:

First, there is what is sometimes called the 'Cathedral' (or 'People's') Office. This is characterized by set rather than serial psalmody, hymnody, short bible lections, a strong accent on intercessions, and a certain amount of ceremonial. At evening, this would include the sharing of light ceremonially, together with the offering of incense (with Psalm 141, which refers directly to incense).

Secondly, there is the 'Monastic' Office, which is longer, reads the Psalter in almost continuous fashion, has longer bible readings (at some services), much less intercession, and is more austere.

Thirdly, there is the Vigil. This is special evening service on Saturdays and the eves of certain important festivals. It usually involves the reading of the resurrection Gospel, or some other Gospel. It is easy to see that the Easter Vigil liturgy, with its complex unfolding of light, word, baptism and Eucharist is but an Easter version of this 'vigil'. Right at the end of the fourth century, we read an account of this latter in the travel-diary of Egeria, the nun who took such care to write down what she saw on her extended holiday in the Eastern Mediterranean:

> At four o'clock they have Lychnicon, as they call it, or in our language, Lucernare. All the people congregate once more in the Anastasis, and the lamps and candles are all lit, which makes it very bright. The fire is brought not from outside, but from the cave – inside the screen – where a lamp is always burning bright night and day. For some time they have the Lucernare psalms and antiphons; then they send for the bishop, who enters and sits in the chief seat. The presbyters also come and sit in their places and the hymns and antiphons go on . . .

> But on the seventh day, the Lord's Day, there gather in the courtyard before cock-crow all the people, as many as can get in, as if it was Easter . . .
>
> Soon the first cock crows, and at that the bishop enters, and goes into the cave in the Anastasis [i.e. the main church]. The doors are all opened, and all the people come into the Anastasis, which is already ablaze with lamps. When they are inside, a psalm is said by one of the presbyters, with everyone responding, and it is followed by a prayer; then a psalm is said by one of the deacons, and another prayer; then a third psalm is said by one of the clergy, a third prayer, and the Commemoration of All [a form of intercession]. After these three psalms and prayers they take censers into the cave of the Anastasis, so that the whole Anastasis is filled with the smell. Then the bishop, standing inside the screen, takes the Gospel book and goes to the door, where he himself reads the account of the Lord's resurrection.
>
> (J.Wilkinson, *Egeria's Travels to the Holy Land*, pp. 124–5)

Here we have in a developed form the evening service, preceded by the *Lucernare*, as Egeria knew it back home on the Atlantic seaboard. Very early next morning (cockcrow in the Middle East is considerably earlier than in this country) the vigil takes place, with the offering of incense, the lamps and candles still lit, and the bishop reads the account of the resurrection. It is easy to see the link with the Easter Vigil, and in time both vigils became anticipated, so that they were celebrated *in toto* late on the Saturday night. The two services can be outlined as follows:

Vespers
- Lighting of the lamps
- Vesperal psalms, including Psalm. 140 (141)
- Antiphons
- Entrance of the bishop
- Hymns or antiphons
- Intercessions and blessing
- Dismissal

Vigil
- Three antiphons with collects in honour of the resurrection on the third day
- General intercessions
- Incensing
- Easter Gospel
- Procession to the cross

What undoubtedly surprises the contemporary reader is the absence of long biblical lections, which were a feature of the monastic services Egeria witnessed, as well as the special popular services on certain occasions, such as Holy Week. It is perhaps a sobering reminder that in the early Church *doxology* – praise – was the fundamental background to all worship, and while there certainly were 'services of instruction', people were quite content to go to church for an act of worship that did not contain a bible reading. Sobering, too, for us who live with the Eucharist so readily available and frequently celebrated is the plain fact that many of our forebears in the faith could attend a simple, repetitive and ceremonious service that was not eucharistic. It is for these and other reasons that the Service of Light has been incorporated into the new book.

Other contemporary and later evidence points to several main trends. The light ceremonies have variable prayers surrounding them, and also (in the West) variable *hymns*, such as was the case at Arles in the time of Caesarius (mid sixth century). A slight tug-of-war is discernible concerning the essential public character of worship when the First Council of Toledo (400) insists that the *Lucernare* can only take place in church, and in the presence of a bishop, presbyter, or deacon. (That must have meant that there were places in which the old vespers persisted in a domestic and lay setting.) Of course, local variations continued and in the Ethiopic Church today there is a gospel lesson early on in vespers, some time before the *Lucernare*, which takes place in the middle. And the monks did not impose a strict austere 'monastic' office everywhere they went; for example, the monks at Bethlehem kept the old 'Cathedral' ('People's') vesperal structure, consisting of *Lucernare* and hymn, Psalm 140 (141) with incense, and intercessions.

The study of comparative liturgy nowadays involves looking at the origins and development of any rite (or part of a rite) in order to distinguish between the 'deep structures' and the 'surface structures'. The deep structures are the original forms and forces at work, and occasionally these can be obscured by a later age coming along and setting things to right in a fit of what we would call relevance. On the other hand, it is possible to encounter a rite or part of a rite that has remained virtually unchanged as a result of 'arrested evolution'. Such indeed has been the case in Milan with the Ambrosian vespers, which, contrary to all moves (suggested and actual) to alter with the times, has remained virtually unchanged through the centuries. The result is that this old 'Cathedral'/'People's' Office on Saturdays maintains in adapted form the medieval synthesis of vespers and vigil, starting with the *Lucernare* and moving on to the resurrection Gospel, so that the essential meaning of the service is a reminder of baptism, thus linking this vigil with the Great Easter Vigil. At a time when baptism is under considerable pressure from the consumer market (whether that be in the form of folk who want to renew their baptism or recommit themselves to Jesus in some way) here is a vital part of Catholic tradition that, if suitably adapted, could serve an important need. It is no coincidence that in such a source as the 1978 *Lutheran Book of Worship* (USA) this sort of rite is to be found, with *Lucernare* leading into evening prayer. *The Promise of His Glory* is part of a general move shared by other churches in the same family.

The Service of Light that appears in the new book takes up the same structure that we have seen in the historic evidence, and while the thanksgiving prayers are modelled as regards shape on the one contained in Hippolytus' *Apostolic Tradition*, the actual content of the several versions varies. Some (e.g. All Saints) are entirely fresh compositions, based on obvious scriptural and other sources, while others (e.g. Advent, no. 2) are adapted from such service books as that of the Taizé community.

The actual content of the 'Word' in these Services of Light can be made up either of the resurrection Gospel, with its rich symbolism, or else one or other of the sequences of readings for carol services; and several of these are included. These repay careful study. Some will appear at first sight to be unusual, but the 'Nine Lessons and Carols' service is really a recent phenomenon and it could be argued that its use of Scripture is not only too demanding on most people today but makes no concessions to biblical scholarship, because of the mixed theology resulting from such a mélange of Scripture. Although this scheme is included, it is hoped that the others will serve to enrich the pre-Christmas and post-Christmas seasons. Perhaps most important of all is the principle that only one lection from the Gospels is read at one service. This has the advantage of familiarizing people with other parts of the Bible, and of not 'spoiling' the other gospel lections at a solemn season when there will be other opportunities to hear them. And this brings in another corrective that *The Promise of His Glory* is attempting to give the Church today, which is to help people *phase* their religious observances, rather than pander to the notion that it is all really a question of concentrating as much as possible into one single service, like drinking concentrated fruit juice. We cannot help being creatures of our own culture, which is why we need to identify those attitudes that we have simply by virtue of living at the time that we do. And having identified them, we can then go on and see where they are conducive to Christian worship, and where they are less so. Using these services may take careful 'selling' at first, because people are at their most conservative on special occasions. (This proves the liturgical 'law' observed by the German liturgist, Anton Baumstark, that liturgy is most resistant to change on solemn feasts and fasts!)

II

The Promise of His Glory discusses the Service of Light and the Vigil Readings right at the beginning since they form a key part of all the different seasonal observances. For most Anglicans in England today the only service in which light is solemnly kindled and shared is the Easter Vigil. Although that is a very limited experience, the Easter Liturgy does give us the Service of Light *par excellence*, and does show that in Christian worship the lighted candle does stand for something. There is a lot of unthinking sentiment attached to candlelight in worship today. The Easter Vigil may be the only time people see it kindled, blessed and shared, but a lot of worship at Christmas can be 'by candlelight' – posters outside churches proclaim it to help draw in the crowds. Yet there is no identification of the light with Jesus Christ; it is simply there as a mood-setter. The task of the Church is not to despise a culture that has taken to candlelight as a kind of holy luxury in an age of instant electric lighting, dimmers and all, but to christianize the light, to kindle it, bless it and share it as a potent symbol of the Lord who is Light and Life.

What the Commission is proposing is that the kindling of light at evening worship should be restored as something Christians regularly do, that it should be part of the ordinary rhythm of worship, as it has become once again in other places. Quietly on Saturday night when the faithful few gather to say Evening Prayer to prepare for Sunday, on Sunday night at Evensong or at the beginning of a service of Prayer and Praise, on the vigils of festivals, and on other occasions when it makes pastoral sense. By providing seasonal blessing prayers it encourages the use of the Service of Light at special liturgies, such as Advent Sunday, Christmas and Candlemas, but that is not as important as encouraging its returning use as a matter of course at the beginning of evening worship.

One note at the end of the introduction to Chapter 2 in *The Promise of His Glory* needs highlighting. It reads:

> The Light: This may be a large candle, or a cluster of candles, set near the Lectern (especially in Eastertide, the Paschal Candle), or the candles of the Holy Table. On certain occasions, it may be appropriate for the congregation to hold candles.

A Service of Light need not, as a matter of course, mean issuing candles to everybody. That would, except on a few occasions, be to give this rite too high a profile. In most circumstances it will be sufficient to light the candles of the sanctuary, if possible without bringing up the electric lighting till that is done. Ideally the main candle or candles should be near the lectern if what is to follow is a Word Service. Even if only in a symbolic way, the Scriptures are to be read by the candle light. There are, of course, occasions when the whole congregation will be given candles to share the light, and these would normally be those services where the service is continued without artificial lighting.

Although the whole chapter in *The Promise of His Glory* is entitled 'The Service of Light', there are in fact three sections to it, all of which can be used independently: Service of Light, Vigil of Readings, Gospel Proclamation. Each needs to be considered in turn.

The Service of Light, or *Lucernare*, may precede any evening worship. Ideally it is celebrated at dusk. As *Phos hilaron* says:

> Now we have come to the setting of the sun.

Very often, though, the service will be celebrated well into the hours of darkness. Although there is no deep reason why it should not be attached to an evening Eucharist where the collect of the day would conclude the *Lucernare*, it is with Word Services and office and vigil structures that it works best. 'Word Services' is here to be understood very widely, as it is in the Liturgical Commission's *Patterns for Worship*. The Service of Light can provide a reflective and joyful beginning to a very informal service, in the Prayer and Praise style, as people sit around the candle and hear the Scriptures read in their midst. There is no need for the lections at a service that follows the Service of Light to be from the Vigil provision here. After the Service of Light, people may return, for instance, to the psalmody and lections for Evening Prayer that day, and this is probably the most common way the service will be used.

A note mentions the role of a deacon. It is the deacon who, in the tradition, blesses the Paschal Candle at the Easter Liturgy in the singing of the *Exultet*. The Blessing of Light in this rite is always a little *Exultet*, and in a Church where there are now many deacons it is appropriate for them to fulfil this liturgical ministry. *The Promise of His Glory* does, at various new points, allow for a minister other than the president. In this respect it is more flexible than the ASB. (The Dismissal at the end of the Eucharist is another such point.)

The singing of *Phos hilaron* is not absolutely necessary to the rite, and a list notes a whole set of alternative light hymns, some of them with seasonal bias, and some more from the chorus culture than traditional hymnody. Nevertheless there is something incomparably apt about *Phos hilaron*, and it is simply a matter of finding the version and tune that work in a particular community, or, better still, having several within the repertoire. Keble's 'Hail, gladdening light', with Stainer's tune 'Sebaste' (AMNS 8), seems to be out of fashion at present, and that is a pity. Robert Bridges' 'O gladsome light' (NEH 247) was the ASB's preferred option. *Hymns for Today's Church* gives an easier version, Christopher Idle's 'Light of gladness' (HTC 277), which is sung to 'Quem pastores'.

After the Service of Light, the chapter next provides patterns for readings, with psalms, canticles and collects. This is one of the great resource sections of the book, with seventeen sets of readings with complementary material, each with its own theme that belongs within the All Saints to Candlemas period. Two of these seventeen are a little different from the others, one because it reads through Luke 1 and 2 in a series of consecutive readings, the other because it provides the customary readings for the Service of Nine Lessons and Carols made popular by King's College Cambridge. The other fifteen have a common style: five readings from the Old Testament, one from the Epistles, psalmody after each, a scriptural canticle, a gospel reading and a collect.

There are occasions and places where these will be used just as they stand. But this is resource material, and people must pick and choose and adapt. Not many parish communities will sustain a service musically dominated by psalms and canticles. Hymns and choruses may take their place, though it would be an impoverishment if all the psalmody and canticle material were jettisoned. Not every service calls for a format that leads only to a single time of prayer at the end. No matter, the minister simply brings into his draft additional times of prayer, even, for instance, a collect after each reading. It will all depend on the occasion for which he is devising worship. He has been provided with outline material that will allow him to devise a grand Advent Liturgy, a quiet half hour instead of Evening Prayer on the

Eve of St Andrew to pray for mission, an Epiphany Carol Service, an all-night vigil for the local branch of Amnesty International. He has to exercise choice and use imagination.

The final section of the chapter is 'The Gospel Proclamation'. This simple order is built around the gospel reading, with acclamations, canticle, prayer and blessing. Where a full Vigil Service has been celebrated it will form a natural climax, but its use extends beyond this, most obviously to Evening Prayer on Saturdays and on the eve of festivals. Whether the Service of Light has been used at the beginning of the service or not, whether Vigil Readings have been read or not, a Saturday night service, or a service on the night before a feast, appropriately ends with the reading of tomorrow's Gospel as a preparation for the festival.

To understand the Light Service + Vigil + Gospel pattern in *The Promise of His Glory* is to have taken on board one of its most important underlying structures. In services as different as a Service to Commemorate the Faithful Departed or in a Christmas Christingle, that structure is just below the surface. It is there because it is proving to have a satisfying shape and development, like that of the Eucharist itself.

THREE

All Saintstide

I

God the Father Almighty, of whom the whole family in heaven and earth is named; Vouchsafe unto you and unto all His saints the fulness of joy from His presence, and the treasures of goodness from His right hand.

The Lord Jesus Christ, who hath so loved the Church that He hath given Himself for it, and nourished and cherished it, even as His own Body; Cleanse and sanctify, nourish and strengthen you, and all them that are His; and keep you spotless and blameless, that he may present you in the unity of the one Body, without fault, before the throne of God.

The Holy Ghost, the Spirit of holiness that dwelleth in the Body, the Church, conform you to the image of Christ the Lord, from glory to glory; and inspire you with the love of God, that ye may abound in hope toward God, and toward all His saints.

God Almighty, the Father, the Son, and the Holy Ghost, keep and bless you, and all His saints, living and departed; and bring you all unto eternal life, in the glory of the resurrection. Amen.

These words read like a mixture between the new seasonal blessings that can be used at the end of the Eucharist in the 1970 Roman Missal and those episcopal blessings that used to be given to non-communicants just before they left church in the old Frankish Church. But they actually belong to the nineteenth century. The blessing concerned was written in 1875 for use on All Saints' Day in the Catholic Apostolic ('Irvingite') Church, a Church that produced an interesting liturgy, but has since died away. The prayer – and others like it – was inspired by the practice of the early medieval Church, although the actual text is a subtle interweaving of biblical allusions and piety. It may perhaps prove the law of liturgical composition, that there is nothing new under the sun (Ecclesiastes 1.9)! The method behind that prayer's construction seems to be exactly the same as that of many twentieth-century texts, a creative and adaptative use of a traditional model.

But what of the meaning of the text? It is strong in trinitarian theology, something that has been out of fashion for some time but, one senses, is coming back into vogue. It is strong on the *fact* of sanctification, and its consequences. It is strong on the ecclesial character of the new community, that those who are Christians are part of a fellowship that is considerably larger than our own churchy back-gardens. It is strong on the groundwork themes such as spiritual growth, holiness, and union with Christ. It makes the purposes of God as revealed in the saints something *accessible* to people. And by bringing *all* the saints into the orbit of present redemption, it brings home to the Church here and now that it has the authority both to bless the *whole* community and to pray for the *whole* community's ultimate and final redemption – in the resurrection. Those final words perhaps hark back to the concluding portion of the Prayer for the Church in the 1549 Prayer Book (sadly lost in 1552, but restored in the Scottish liturgies from 1637 onwards) which runs, 'Come ye, blessed of my Father, inherit the Kingdom prepared for you from the foundation of the world.'

Many modern service books do contain seasonal blessings, though not in quite as lengthy a form as the one quoted. But more important, there is a trend discernible in the kind of compositions that are now being put together in the aftermath of official liturgical revision to restore to worship something of the heavenly dimension. There is an old Orthodox tag that the liturgy is 'playing at heaven'. Whatever one thinks of the length and historic character of Orthodox worship, one has to admit that its sense of timelessness does judge some of the modern West's more introspective liturgical performances in recent years. One thinks of celebrations where there appears to be no president, for fear of being authoritarian, and in which the intercessions are a sort of orgy of self-pity, in which the faithful wallow in not having changed the face of the world completely since they last met, and sermons that are exhortations to greater human effort, where the fact and truth of redemption become conditional on a sort of tired, clapped-out Pelagianism. The millions of people who never go near public worship except for rites of passage, but who flock to our cathedrals and ancient parish churches, are, surely, the very people who are reaching out for something else. Someone once told me quite firmly that it is no wonder that so many young people indulged in black magic and spiritualism, when the Church had lost interest in heaven.

The origins of All Saints' Day are about as straightforward as a bent spring. Ephrem the Syrian (who died in 373) mentions the practice of commemorating all the martyrs, but he does not say exactly when in the course of the year. The Syriac Breviary (a document from about the same area, and the same time) states that the martyrs were commemorated in April. But at the start of the fifth century, John Chrysostom tells us that all the saints have their collective day on the first Sunday after Pentecost; and that is where they still are in the Byzantine rite all over the world today. (It is ironical that the West should in the later Middle Ages make *that* day the feast of the Holy Trinity, thus marking another and quite different theological priority.) The background of martyrs, and the Church of the persecuted, are perhaps reflected in the Troparion for this occasion in the Byzantine Church:

> O Christ God, your Church, crimsoned with the blood of your martyrs all over the world as with a cloak of murex and porphyry, cries out to You: 'Send your mercy upon your people, grant peace to your fold, and extend your great compassion upon our souls.'
>
> (*Byzantine Daily Worship*, Tournai, Desclée, 1967, p. 906)

And the Gospel, a curious compendium (Matthew 10.32–8 and 19.27–30), is about the cost of discipleship.

The feast gradually came West, through the inevitable trade route. Pope Boniface IV consecrated the old pagan Pantheon on 13 May, and on that day the martyrs remained. However, in the middle of the next century, Gregory III (d. 741) dedicated a chapel in St Peter's Basilica to All Saints, and Gregory IV (d. 844) established its universal observance. Pope Sixtus IV (d. 1484) gave it an Octave, thus according it the kind of accolade which only a very important feast deserves. The standard Gospel in the West is the beginning of the Sermon on the Mount in the Matthean version (Matthew 5.1ff.) The various prayers and hymns in use in the medieval West are clearly about all the saints, not just the martyrs. But we must remember that all through the Middle Ages local saints were constantly arriving on the scene, and extra saints' days were being added to the calendar. It is only really with the advent of the Lutheran and Anglican Calendars at the Reformation that All Saints' Day could stand out in such prominence, since only a few of the individual saints' days had survived the theological pruning to which the medieval service-books were subjected. It is interesting to note that the ASB Calendar, following other Anglican calendars, makes 8 November, the Octave day of All Saints, the day for the commemoration of national saints and martyrs.

All Souls' Day, on the other hand, has a different history altogether. Odilo of Cluny in AD 998 imposed its observance on 2 November on all Benedictine communities. Already, Masses offered for the dead were a prominent feature of monastic houses, for in the preceding century, numerous types of such mass texts were written and arranged for inclusion in the official Sacramentaries and (later) Missals. It would not be an oversimplification to say that the Byzantine Calendar looks at all the saints, but particularly the martyrs. (Coming straight after Pentecost, the Byzantine liturgical year would perhaps move easily from the foundation of the Church in Acts 2 to the martyrdom of Stephen in Acts 6ff.) Then, the Roman Church looks at all the saints as the embodiment of the life of the beatitudes. Later, as part of its response to the medieval preoccupation with death and the after-life, it colours its own Calendar with the consequences of an increasingly elaborate series of funeral rites. It was inevitable, natural, and open to misunderstanding and abuse.

At the Reformation, the Calvinists and Zwinglians got rid of funeral rites and the Church Year altogether. The Lutherans and Anglicans, on the other hand, produced drastically simplified funeral liturgies, got rid of All Souls' Day, but kept All Saints' Day. But not all the Reformers lost their sense of worship in heaven, thanksgiving for those who have gone before us, and the promise of redemption, as this much-undervalued hymn by Richard Baxter (1615–91) shows:

He wants not friends that hath thy love,
And may converse and walk with thee,
And with thy saints here and above,
With whom for ever I must be.

In the blest fellowship of saints
Is wisdom, safety, and delight:
And when my heart declines and faints,
It's raisèd by their heat and light.

As for my friends, they are not lost;
The several vessels of thy fleet,
Though parted now, by tempests tost,
Shall safely in thy haven meet.

Still we are centred all in thee,
Members, though distant, of one Head;
In the same family we be,
By the same faith and spirit led.

Before thy throne we daily meet
As joint-petitioners to thee;
In spirit we each other greet,
And shall again each other see.

The heavenly hosts, world without end,
Shall be my company above;
And thou, my best and surest Friend,
Who shall divide me from thy love?

Baxter apparently wrote these remarkably sensitive stanzas 'when I was silenced and cast out', probably at a time when as a young pastor he was working without much reward. But thank goodness for the conditions of his soul that produced such a hymn! For the sentiments and thought-structure prove beyond any doubt that the Reformers were not by any means anti-saint, least of all those High Church Puritans who combined a simple style of worship with a strong doctrine of sacraments and the importance of worship. But for all of that, there *is* a Reformation protest, and no service book produced even for optional use by the Church of England can ignore it.

The liturgical protest has already been described. All

Souls' Day and medieval funeral rites are suspect because of what they do and say. The *theological* protest is about dividing those who have died neatly into two separate camps, those who are saints, about whom we are certain, and who pray for us, and those about whom we must remain agnostic, who are in purgatory, and for whom we must pray. Granted that purgatory is a relatively late arrival on the scene, a belief in purgatory underlies many of the attitudes that ordinary people brought with them to funerals and requiem Masses. Although the 1549 Prayer Book kept provision for the Eucharist at a funeral, that provision disappeared in 1552. And yet we know that the Eucharist was indeed celebrated during Queen Elizabeth I's reign when certain notable people died. We are here seeing a sort of Catholic survival, in a mild form, for the classical Anglican tradition of the seventeenth century held strongly to the union of the living and departed in Christ, a union directly alluded to in the Prayer for the whole state of Christ's Church.

But the problem is really a very Western one, which has in the past insisted on looking in absolute terms at the saints-versus-departed controversy in too precise a manner. The Eastern view has never worked that way. I think it can help us.

It seems more helpful and more faithful to the gospel if we approach this issue by looking at the matter *from our own context* rather than *from where 'they' are*. At All Saints' Day, we rejoice in the glory of God manifested in the lives of human beings, and that means the great heroes of the whole Church, as well as the more local figures which every nation has. This is one of the reasons why the Thanksgiving for the Holy Ones of God forms an important part of the All Saints' Day rites. We are not worshipping ideas; we are giving thanks fundamentally for what *God* has done. Then on All Souls' Day, our context is different. A particular group of people remember particular people whom they remember, mainly those whom they knew in this life, or else heard about. Many people come to commemoration services, either at anniversaries (sometimes very tender occasions) or else at All Souls. They do not think their prayers are in some way remitting spells of purgation or anything so crude as that. But they want to remember, to cry, to pray, to pay respects. And that is why reading out lists of names is often a helpful way of bringing home the reality of death, and the reality of the Christian promise. At another level altogether, and in a different context, Remembrance Sunday provides a similar opportunity. These are issues that cannot be dismissed in a dogmatic sermon. They are matters that need constantly to be ritualized.

In the provisions for these days, All Saints follows this line of reasoning. As fellow-Christians with the saints, we are one in faith (Hebrews 2.1–2), one in anticipation (Revelation 6.10), and one in praise (Hebrews 12.22–3). These are basic biblical truths, and if handled carefully and thoughtfully should serve to rid some Anglicans of that unhelpful Reformation instinct that tends to regard saints as an irrelevance. Two particular texts for All Saints underscore these rich, biblical themes. One is the Intercession, taken from the Coptic anaphora (eucharistic prayer) of Basil of Caesarea, which speaks of those who are 'well-pleasing from eternity'. Another is the Post-Communion Prayer, taken from the Catholic Apostolic rite, with its strong imagery of the eucharistic table on earth and its relationship with the heavenly banquet itself. The option to observe All Saints' Day on a *Sunday*, as is suggested, was also a Catholic Apostolic custom, and will surely help to bring this festival into the prominence it rightly deserves.

Among the other items in the book is a fine Proper Preface for use at the Eucharist which is based on the start of the Te Deum, thus at last providing an official place for that ancient hymn within the eucharistic prayer, where some scholars believe it to have been born in any case. We have also included a version of the thirteenth-century Latin hymn, *Dies irae*, which (as it happens) was written in the first person, for use during Advent, and was therefore intended for individual devotional use, not for popular and public recitation. One wonders what the author would make of some of the contexts and settings in which it has been sung down the ages! The theological point made earlier about seeing our way through the Reformation controversy by looking at it from the point of view of context is, in fact, proved by the hymns that have been written on the All Saints'–All Souls' themes in recent years. It is no longer possible to drive a wedge, *theologically*, between the two occasions, and I doubt if the first Benedictine users of All Souls' Day texts did either. It would seem that theological correctives are around us. But there is one overwhelming reason for adopting in some form these observances. People today need a sense of identity and history. Somehow, the Orthodox have managed to keep that dimension. We Westerners may not be able to identify with it in all its manifestations. But saints help to give a local and universal Church a sense of continuity and story. Edward King, who was the saintly Bishop of Lincoln at the turn of the century, is still talked about. When I was first ordained, some of the elderly parishioners I used to visit in his former diocese would speak about him as if he had only just left. To praise God in union with all the saints is to join ourselves with them, as we await the end of all things. Just because many features of modern living make that kind of approach one that requires further thought and explanation should not disable us from approaching the throne of grace through living history. As with so many areas of Christian truth, it is not so much a matter of seeing something important because it is good therapy ('It makes us feel better') as because without it our understanding of the nature of the Church is faulty ('Who shall divide me from thy love?'). Above all, the fundamental message of All Saintstide is to point to the eschatological nature of the Christian faith, an emphasis which runs the risk in a consumer-orientated society with its love of fine management of being submerged under a vague guise of 'do-gooding' religiosity. The blessing quoted at the beginning of this chapter is a firm reminder that this dimension not only belongs to us in November, but prepares us for the following month of Advent.

II

The words of the introduction to this chapter of *The Promise of His Glory* are crucial. The Commission states:

> We have included provision for this season partly for the practical reason that it falls within the period of the year we are covering and has implications for the calendar in the pre-Advent period, but mainly because there is an important theological connection between our celebration of the saints and our reflection on God's Judgement on us. In other words, All Saints' and Advent belong together, and the one informs the other.

That theological emphasis needs to be taken on board before the observance of the whole pre-Christmas season can be planned. All Saintstide is seen as one of two neglected pivot points in the year (the other is Candlemas) where the liturgy changes direction quite dramatically. Put very simply, the white/gold feast of All Saints comes at the end of the long season of Pentecost green. All Souls' Day, the Commemoration of the Faithful Departed, with its purple vestments, begins a darker season that will take us on to Christmas.

But, of course, it is not as simple as that. It is not as simple as that partly because neither BCP nor ASB calendars give All Saints' Day that pivotal function. The Prayer Book is still ploughing through its Sundays after Trinity. The ASB has abandoned 'Sundays after Pentecost' the week before and is by now on Sundays before Christmas, looking at The Fall. This is not very tidy, but while these provisions have to exist alongside the ASB, as well as the Prayer Book, we have to live with them. The calendar sets out how to make the transfer from the ASB lectionary to this one in time to give All Saints' Day its significant place, and this is set out carefully at the end of Chapter 1 of *The Promise of His Glory*. Briefly the ASB calendar is abandoned after what it calls 'The Last Sunday after Pentecost'. The final Sunday in October, which is a kind of spare Sunday before entering the new cycle, may be kept in a variety of different ways depending on local circumstances:

> It may be kept as the Dedication Festival where the real date is unknown or unsuitable. This is instead of present provision to do this on the first Sunday in October, often mixed up with Harvest.

It may be kept as Reformation Sunday, as in the Lutheran tradition, and given a particular emphasis on the Word of God revealed in Scripture. This would take the pressure off Advent 2, which at present finds itself trying to be a Bible Sunday at the same time as holding the Advent line against the encroachment of the pre-Christmas festivities.

It may be kept as a Justice and Peace Sunday, picking up on the One World Week and Week of Prayer for World Peace that are kept in late October.

It could be simply another Sunday after Pentecost, using a spare set of propers from one of the unused neutral green Sundays.

By one of these means or another, the ground can be laid for the new start to be made, not with a Ninth Sunday before Christmas, but with All Saints' Day, which may be kept on 1 November itself, or on a Sunday between 31 October and 7 November.

How the season continues is discussed below. Meanwhile we turn to the material provided for All Saints' Day.

The Eucharist of All Saints' Day provides a series of texts that enrich the rite on this day, but there is no special feature to the rite in a way that there is for some other feasts. One area that needs decision locally is whether to include a penitential section. The rite, as it stands, has quite a powerful intercessory section that leads naturally into the Greeting of Peace introduced by the words:

> May the God of peace make *you* perfect and holy, that you may be kept safe and blameless in spirit, soul and body, for the coming of our Lord Jesus Christ.

Penitence would be an intrusion between those. Equally it would destroy the fine responsory at the beginning to insert penitence between that responsory and the Gloria. With both the conventional places for confession unsuitable, the rubrics allow its omission altogether, or its positioning in a fairly brief form before the Intercession Prayers.

There are three features that are common to several of the main eucharistic liturgies in *The Promise of His Glory*, and which the reader first meets in relation to this All Saints' Day rite. The first is a bidding and a suggestion of silence before the collect. This is a conscious attempt to restore the idea of the collect as the prayer that sums up and draws together the silent prayer that each person should make at this point. In some ways the suggested, 'Let us pray that we may be strengthened by our communion with all the saints', is too restrictive. People simply need to be invited to pray; they do not, on the whole, need to be told exactly what to pray. But the Commission has taken the line that the bald 'Let us pray' has become so confused with an instruction about posture, and that the idea of silent prayer at this point is so novel to most Anglicans, that a more helpful bidding is needed. The hope must be that, if people grow used to the 'Bidding-Silence-Collect' formula at All Saintstide, Christmas, Candlemas and so on, they will learn to expect and to use such provision at every Eucharist. Once the point has been assimilated, the collect without bidding and silence feels a real impoverishment.

The second feature common to several of the rites is the special intercession, often with guidance about how material is to be inserted. In the liturgical revision of the 1960s and 1970s people welcomed the opportunity to 'loosen up' intercessory prayer from the strait-jacket of the Intercession at Holy Communion in the Book of Common Prayer. But there is now a need perceived on special occasions for an intercession form that rises above the ordinary, is richer in its language, and breaks away from a style that has become rather fixed in many churches. The Intercession for All Saints' Day is a fine example of this. Its themes are relevant to the particular day, the material in it relates to other parts of the day's liturgy, scriptural imagery is employed, the language has a poetic quality to it, and the ending leads in a very natural way into the Greeting of Peace.

The danger, of course, is that in the hands of someone with insufficient sensitivity it will be ruined by interpolation, as if it were just the ordinary Rite A Sunday text designed for such consumer input. But we are dealing here with a form that has a shape and a rhythm of its own that cannot sustain long sentences or lists of names within it. They are not necessarily to be excluded from the day's liturgy, but they need to be given in the form of biddings before the set prayer begins. For some people who have only led prayer in the Rite A interpolation style this is new, and they will need help with it.

The final feature common to several of the rites is the Solemn Blessing. These blessings have their origin in the Gallican/Visigothic rite, and found their way into the Roman rite via the Gelasian Sacramentaries. But in every case the texts have been newly composed, the Roman ones having been found wanting. A Solemn Blessing on a limited number of occasions marks out particular days as significant and special. It enables a richer series of ideas to be employed than in a simple blessing. And, with the repeated congregational 'Amen', it becomes, in a sense, a kind of responsory. The All Saints' Day one is, in a way, the least typical in this book since it does not have the strict trinitarian shape of the others. Nevertheless it brings together in the final words of the service marvellous truths that have been celebrated and which may be received as a blessing. It is a strong ending.

Though the Eucharist will nearly always be the principal celebration of All Saints' Day, there will sometimes be room for other material, especially when the festival is kept on the Sunday, instead of, or in addition to, 1 November itself. The 'Thanksgiving for the Holy Ones of God', based on a Franciscan original, but substantially rewritten by the Commission, partly to make it more of a celebration of sanctity today as well as in the past, and partly to redress the balance in terms of the heroic sanctity of women, provides an excellent litany form for a non-eucharistic service, and a rubric directs helpfully how to use it at Morning or Evening Prayer. Its Visigothic concluding prayer

> May the infinite and glorious Trinity, the Father, the Son, and the Holy Spirit, direct our life in good works, and after our journey through this world, grant us eternal rest with the saints

deserves to be drawn into more common currency, and not just on 1 November.

2 November is the day of the Commemoration of the Faithful Departed. That title, which the ASB employs, is used

in *The Promise of His Glory*, in preference to the more common 'All Souls' Day' out of sensitivity to those, among Evangelicals, who have some difficulty with prayer for the departed. But the choice of title is not just a gesture. It represents a genuine effort by the Commission members to find new common ground among people of different theological traditions about what we may say about our relationship with the Christian dead. The truce that shaped the language of the ASB Funeral Service, for instance, has meant that no conscience need be offended, but it has been at the price of fairly bland and impoverished language for the communion of saints. In a number of ways *The Promise of His Glory* tries to move the subject on, seeking language that is richer, but which will unite Christians rather than divide them. This has been achieved partly by a renewed emphasis on the eschatological nature of All Saintstide. As quoted above, 'All Saints and Advent belong together.'

At various times – not least at the time of the English Reformation – people have thought that, for theological reasons, All Souls should disappear and leave All Saints' Day to celebrate the totality of the communion of the saints, without any of the dangers, described above, of categorizing the departed. But *The Promise of His Glory* recognizes the need to remember our *own* departed, in a more local and personal way, the need to grieve, and the need to reflect soberly on the judgement of God. Arising from that, it has made the Commemoration of All Souls the occasion to begin the Advent mood. Such outward features as the omission of the Gloria and the use of purple or blue vestments, once established on 2 November, remain through till Advent gives way to Christmas. How the weeks between 2 November and Advent Sunday are to be handled is discussed in the next chapter. Sufficient to say here that All Souls is not, in this calendar, an isolated 'purple' day, but the beginning of a new mood and season.

'2 November' must, of course, mean '2 November or soon after'. It would not make sense to have this move to the purple mood before All Saints' Day had been kept. If All Saints is transferred to a Sunday, The Commemoration of the

Faithful Departed must follow on the first convenient day. Exactly when these days are celebrated must be decided locally, with an understanding of the liturgical principles, but also with sound pastoral judgement, not least because this season has so much potential for ministry to the bereaved.

All Saintstide comes just at the time when leaves have fallen, clocks have been put back and the long dark evenings have begun. Pastorally this can be the right moment for an invitation to those who have been bereaved to come to church to remember their dead. An increasing number of parishes are doing this, keeping a careful record of those to whom the parish has ministered in the previous year or so at the time of the death of a loved one, and inviting them now to a service to remember and pray. The Eucharist for The Commemoration of the Faithful Departed is designed so that it may be used for such a service, and there is also a non-eucharistic alternative. Where invitations like this are being used, the services are being found to meet a real need, and it must be hoped that the publication of *The Promise of His Glory* will encourage more parishes to find a way to use this season to reach out beyond their regular congregations.

The eucharistic rite itself is fairly straightforward, except for the particular feature of the Commemoration, which needs to be looked at with some care. Prayers of penitence are placed near the beginning, not only because the Intercession once again leads naturally into the Peace, but also because this seems to be one of the occasions when people often come with some initial unburdening to do.

The Commemoration is printed after Communion, though a rubric allows it an earlier point before the Prayers of Intercession. The Commission opted for the latter position because, theologically, it wanted to bring communion and commemoration together. It is at the altar in our communion that we come closest not only to our Father, but to those whom we have entrusted to him. But the alternative, earlier, position has been allowed for those who feel that something that may be fairly heavily charged emotionally should not come so near the end of the service.

Where the Commemoration takes place after Communion, it is important that it be *immediately* after Communion. The insertion of a hymn, or, worse, a gap while the vessels were cleansed, would undermine the idea of commemoration as an extension of communion. Immediately the Distribution is over, the president should take his place, perhaps standing by the paschal candle, for the Commemoration.

Should there be a long list of names read out? Some, as has been said above, do find it helpful to hear the names of those they love read. In some churches this can create a major problem, where a list of departed relatives of churchgoers, plus a list of parishioners who have died in the last year, could well produce a list of names in three figures.

One solution, and it is mentioned in the service rubrics but perhaps not as strongly as it might, is the lighting of candles. There is no need for a long list if each person is to come forward to light a candle for those whom they have in their hearts. Where churches have done this, people have found it a helpful thing, charged with meaning, to come forward and light a candle before the altar. With a large congregation it takes time, but, in a strange way, what people are doing at that moment *needs* time, and actually benefits from taking time. There needs to be music when there is a large congregation, and the prayer, 'Give rest, O Christ, to your servants . . .' (The Russian Contakion), may well be sung at this point, while the prayer 'Hear us, O merciful Father, as we remember . . .' is best as a congregational prayer after all the candles have been lit.

There will then need to be a strong congregational hymn before the Blessing and Dismissal. The second of the forms of blessing is one that clergy might well use at funerals. The lack of a blessing in the present ASB rite is a serious deficiency in a service when congregations need it the more.

The Dismissal intentionally does not have the 'get up and go' flavour. This is an occasion when people may well want to linger, especially where there are candles they have lit burning before the altar. It is also an occasion when, if the liturgy has touched people deeply as it has the power to do, there will be no takers for the well-intentioned cup of coffee after the service, and it might be better on this day just to let people take time to stay and then leave when they are ready.

There was a time when, if a church was looking for a format to put fringe Christians at ease, it would have fallen back on an Evensong format. Most people today are more confused by that than by the Eucharist, and a new generation of non-communicants is emerging that does not seem ill at ease at the Eucharist. Nevertheless there follows in this chapter of *The Promise of His Glory* a non-eucharistic service to commemorate the faithful departed and this will meet a need on many occasions.

As it stands it moves from an opening rite, that can be a form of *Lucernare,* through a Ministry of the Word and Intercessory Prayer to a Commemoration similar to that in the Eucharist. Material here and in the eucharistic form are, to some extent, interchangeable. More important, what is given here will, with only small adaptation, provide for other quite different occasions and times of the year. The opening rubric notes its possible use on an anniversary or as the basis of a Memorial or Thanksgiving Service. This will, perhaps, be its greatest usefulness, for clergy are often unsure how to set about a Memorial Service that honours the dead but proclaims the Christian gospel effectively. There is also, thankfully, a chance that those who take funerals will draw some of the material here into a funeral service that so desperately needs enrichment.

The chapter ends with provision for Remembrance Sunday. The text provided is not new. It is the one that has been authorized for over twenty years for use ecumenically. The time is ripe for its revision, but this is something that ought properly to be undertaken with the other Christian traditions. Where *The Promise of His Glory* does come to our aid is in providing a calendar and lectionary where the Remembrance theme can be handled and honoured without cutting right across the liturgical development through November. But this is further discussed in the following chapter.

Only in a minority of churches has All Saints' Day, let alone the Commemoration of the Faithful Departed, been fully observed in the past. This has been, at least in part, because they have seemed like islands in a sea of green, not in any kind of communication with anything around them. In what is being provided now, they can be rescued as a telling start to a season that helps us face death with a serious confidence and points us to judgement and yet to heaven.

FOUR

Advent

I

Sleepers wake! the watch-cry pealeth,
While slumber deep each eyelid sealeth:
Awake, Jerusalem, awake!
Midnight's solemn hour is tolling,
And seraph-notes are onward rolling;
They call on us our part to take.
  Come forth, ye virgins wise:
  The Bridegroom comes, arise!
    Alleluia!
  Each lamp be bright
  With ready light
To grace the marriage feast tonight.

So runs the first stanza of Philipp Nicolai's well-known hymn *'Wachet auf, ruft uns die Stimme'* in English translation. He was a son of the Lutheran vicarage, and lived from 1556 to 1608, eventually working at Herdecke and then at the prestigious post of St Katharine's, Hamburg. Unusually, he is both the author of the hymn and the composer of the tune, though the words appear to have been inspired by others written by Hans Sachs, a contemporary of Luther's. Another unusual twist is that in this country we tend to associate it with Advent, whereas the Lutheran world has traditionally associated it with the end of the Church Year, and therefore has sung it before Advent even begins. There are, of course, many Lutheran Advent hymns, and in some respects one of the best features about Advent is that there are so many fine compositions in the repertoire. One thinks of Martin Luther's translation of Ambrose's *'Veni redemptor gentium'*, which begins *'Nun Komm, der Heiden Heiland'*, known well to organists through the chorale preludes written by Bach and Buxtehude.

But it is not for nothing that the hymn is only loosely

connected with Advent, for it makes the necessary eschatological point yet again, namely that the waiting and the watching have to go on. They are not time-locked. They are not programmed by the filofax. And the more haunting the music and the words themselves, the more effective the singing seems to be. North Europeans who live with dark winters have, perhaps, an instinct that wants to hibernate at this time of year. It would seem that even the distractions of preparing for Christmas cannot wake up some Christians, not that Nicolai had much of *that* to cope with in his day! At root, what this hymn rings in is the season of Advent. We may well ask why bother with it, because of three major stumbling-blocks that keep getting in the way, and they have been brought into sharp relief in recent years.

The first problem is that, for most people today, great events are not prepared for at length, and then celebrated in their own right in a prolonged manner. This applies to many areas of life, not just to the way the Church Year is handled, though this has drastic consequences today, as Bryan Spinks has shown. Our forebears kept Advent, and then switched to Christmas, and (in theory at least) celebrated that feast, and the Christmas saints, and Epiphany, and then on 'Twelfth Night' took down the Christmas decorations. We, on the other hand, spend most of Advent (and before) preparing for Christmas, and at the same time anticipating it. It means spending a great deal of Advent rushing from one social–carol event to another. Then when Christmas Day comes along, there appears to be little energy left to extend the celebration further. Everyone packs up thereafter, though some may emerge for Epiphany after the break!

The second problem concerns our attitudes to the future. It is hard for many of us really to believe in a God who has the future in his control, when so many plans are laid, blueprints given, and ideas tried out for what our world, our school, our factory, our office *could* be like *if only* . . . Further, we do live in a world in which many of us immediately feel the consequences of what are in effect the most ridiculous events, such as a mild fluctuation on the Stock Exchange or Wall Street. What has God got to say to that kind of situation?

Third, and related to the first two, there is the modern fad for wanting to be in *control* of situations. How many congregations value a good organizer as a priest more than a man of God or a fine preacher? I wonder how often the current fad for making really tough demands on families who want their babies baptized is in fact the Church reflecting this desire for controlling the future and eliminating the element of risk that is around us nowadays? What sort of God do we look to?

These, and other, matters are crucial questions and they are not to be brushed aside, because they are part of the agenda that people bring with them, as they sit in our churches up and down the country. To the need to celebrate by anticipation, the answer is to make much more of Advent, so that it regains some of its former, more traditional, features of being a time of rejoicing – provided that we give it the space and the resources to do so. That is one of the reasons for producing *The Promise of His Glory*, as was said in an earlier chapter.

To those who look to the future with anxiety and frustration, the answer is to look at the Advent Gospels and see there the God who is himself in the midst of human crisis, decision and catastrophe. God lives in the real world, not the world of our fantasies and ideals, though he would like some of those transformed into an eternal reality. The dreams and plans are important! But they are not the whole story. Advent is, above all, the season of imagination.

And to those who are fearful about the need for control in their lives, the answer is not to look for the heavenly headmaster who will carry the old-fashioned stick ('Why can't the Church take a firm line?' – except when it doesn't suit), but rather to see in all that is around us the essentially provisional character of life on this earth. As I write these words, I have recently taken the funeral of a man who quite suddenly collapsed and died in his fifties of a heart attack. If the event brought home to the local community one thing, it is that however many plans and arrangements are made about the future, we are not in control. For if we are, God ceases to be God. Advent is the time of the God of surprises.

There are, of course, many other Advent problems which

keep recurring. In our own century, the whole belief in the Second Coming has degenerated into a sort of fairy-tale. But one day there *will* be an end to this world – and what do we expect to happen? Philipp Nicolai's hymn warns us that we need to be awake and ready, watching and praying. Another Lutheran hymn, by the Dane, Nikolai Grundtvig, meditates poetically on the scene in Isaiah 35.1–6, and in the middle stands back and asks that the Son of David would accomplish this promise in the desert ('Blomstre som en rosengård').

Like most of the Church Year, Advent began to emerge in the fourth century. In 380, the Council of Saragossa in Spain laid down that Christians should fast from 17 December until Epiphany (then Spain's Christmas festival, as it was in Jerusalem). Filastrius of Brescia, writing about 385, refers to the fast before Christmas, but he does not say how long it should be. In about 542, Caesarius of Arles exhorted his congregation to prepare for their Christmas communion with several days of reflection. A Synod in Tours in 567 directed that monks must fast in December, and in 581 this was extended to include all Christians, so that they fasted on Mondays, Wednesdays and Fridays from 11 November onwards. We have here, therefore, a picture of a penitential preparation for Christmas in France and Spain.

But in Rome, things are not so clear cut. Around this time, it appears that the second half of December was kept as the end of the agricultural year, and that, therefore, Christians interpreted it as a time to celebrate the end of all history, the consummation of all things. Whatever we are to make of this, it would seem that we have already the two slightly conflicting interpretations of the pre-Christmas season. On the one hand, you must be penitent. On the other hand, you must rejoice at the end.

So much for the meaning. What of the length? This has varied considerably. Today, the Copts and Nestorians have a four-week Advent, and the Syrian Jacobites have five Sundays. Milan has six and has had ever since the seventh century, at least. At Rome, there appear to have been six at one time, which was reduced to five (the origin for 'Stir up' Sunday), which in the tenth and eleventh centuries was further reduced to four. History does not settle finally such a disputed and flexible point. The important feature, however, is that Advent, whether penitential or joyous, should look forward to Christmas/Epiphany, in a series of Sunday preparations, however many they may be, and live with the dual expectation of the Infant coming in poverty, and the King coming in majesty.

At the Reformation, the Roman scheme was modified by the Lutheran and Anglican books, but largely taken over, with four Sundays and (as we have already pointed out) the last Sunday after Trinity remaining with its collect and readings that really belonged to the first Sunday of a five-week Advent. Then the ASB scheme came along with nine Sundays before Christmas, of which the last four were to be Advent, in a slightly adapted guise. (This was taken over from the 1967 Joint Liturgical Group proposals.) The trouble with those is that they seem more pedagogical than kerygmatic, and can come across to people as preaching at them instead of proclaiming to them. More important for our purposes here, they altogether lack the traditional flavouring to the beginning of November being brought to the fore in these new services.

The provisions in the new book introduce a different element, namely an adaptation of the three-year Lectionary of the Roman Catholic Church (1970). Once again, at first sight this may cause some surprise, but it must be noted that parts of the Roman Lectionary have been authorized first of all with the ASB (the Daily Eucharistic Lectionary) and secondly with parts of *Lent, Holy Week, Easter: Services and Prayers*. We shall discuss the Lectionary in more detail in a later chapter. For the moment, it is important to realize that *The Promise of His Glory* adopts this lectionary from the Third Sunday before Advent. For those who follow the ASB Lectionary, they may select from provisions in ASB not required after Epiphany or after Pentecost, or they may observe the preceding two Sundays as the Dedication Festival and All Saints' Day Sunday, *The Promise of His Glory's* preferred option.

The new book thus takes another but wider approach to

the Advent season, first of all from the third Sunday before Advent to the Second Sunday in Advent by reflecting on prophetic, apocalyptic and eschatological topics, and then for the remaining two Sundays in Advent preparing for Christmas by 'annunciations'. The three-year scheme enables the local community to get to grips with a greater selection of scripture passages. This ties in with a point made already that it is important for congregations to become more familiar with a wider view of the Bible at this season. The spiritual implications of this move are immense. For too long, people have approached this season as if they were looking at a picture, with foreground and background in perspective. Christians should, rather, be looking at an *icon*, in which the perspectives are *inverted*, so that the onlooker is brought directly into the scene, and is therefore helped to worship. A better diet of Scripture would help this process.

What, then, of the apparent difference in the origins of Advent, penitential in early France and eschatological in Rome? The two moods clearly mixed, although the tendency in recent centuries was for the penitential style to dominate. No *Gloria in excelsis* at the Eucharist obviously is a step in that direction. But later medieval English colour sequences carefully distinguished between Lent and Advent by laying down sackcloth vestments to be used on the former and blue for the latter, a practice followed in many parishes today. Mood is important in liturgy, and it is too neat, logical and wrong simply to equate Advent with Lent. This is especially true of the new lectionaries, which attempt to bring some of the message of the Annunciation into the latter part of Advent, following ancient (and logical) precedent.

As for the provisions themselves, we have already discussed the Vigil with the Service of Light in a previous chapter. Among the special services are the 'Four Last Things', which take up the more personal aspects of eschatology that have evolved down the ages. This may serve as a useful penitential office for Advent. The service based on the Great 'O' antiphons (which, in their original place, used to signal the last few days before Christmas) begins with the Advent responsory, *Rorate coeli* ('Drop down . . .'), which is first found in the *Officia Propria* published in Paris, 1673, and which is a mark of the Neo-Gallican movement in France in its heyday. The 'O' antiphons inspired the composition of the old and much-loved hymn, 'O come, O come, Emmanuel'.

These services are fresh compositions, inspired by the original material, and are intended, unlike Advent carol services, to form the basis of more devotional offices. In the propers for the Eucharist, most of the material is fresh, or again adapted from traditional sources. For example, the second Proper Preface for Advent is taken from the eighth-century Gelasian Sacramentaries, but has been freely altered.

There is, however, one Advent custom which has become increasingly popular in recent years and which requires some elucidation. The *Advent Wreath* is often observed as a ceremony either in church or in the home (or both). It is sometimes a little hard to unravel a complex series of associations but the story runs something like this:

13 December is St Lucy's day in the Roman Calendar and Lucy was a popular saint in the Middle Ages (her name also appears among the list of saints in the Roman Canon, now called Eucharistic Prayer 1). In Nordic countries, it became customary to crown a young girl with a wreath on which were placed four white lit candles and she was called 'S Lucia'. The custom survived the Reformation in many places, even though the connection between candles and Lucy may be originally pagan (light in the middle of winter). Another custom grew up in the Nordic countries in recent centuries of making a wreath of evergreen and placing on it four red candles and lighting them in turn on the four Sundays of Advent. The practice spread beyond the Scandinavian countries (my Danish mother introduced it into our home), though it has been 'improved' by the addition of a fifth and larger (white) candle, which is lit on Christmas Day. We are by now far away from St Lucy and well into simple Advent folk-religion, and a further testimony that the creation of new symbolism in home and church has not died, but is alive and kicking.

II

The Church of England's Liturgical Commission found itself facing the question, 'How long should Advent be?', against the confused and varied historical background already described, and in particular with the most recent experiment of a nine-week lead up to Christmas, originating with the Joint Liturgical Group, but establishing itself in the ASB. As Kenneth Stevenson has said, it has not been an altogether happy experiment. The motive was sound enough. Four Sundays is not very long to proclaim the great Advent themes, especially if late-Advent is taken over almost entirely by Christmas anticipation.

But the nine weeks before Christmas got it wrong (it is easy to say this with hindsight; it seemed an attractive approach at first) partly because nine weeks is just *too* long, and it is bad enough to be told in advertising that there are only fifty shopping days left to Christmas without being told at the same time in church that there are only nine Sundays left to Christmas at the beginning of the autumn half term! It also got it wrong because it was too half-hearted. The green vestments stayed and there were no hints as to how to give this pre-Christmas season its distinctive flavour. But it got it wrong principally because it lengthened the season, not in order to do justice to the traditional Advent eschatological themes, but in order to introduce the whole Old Testament witness in miniature, bounding from Creation and the Fall through Abraham and Moses, with a hint of Noah and Elijah, a mention of a remnant, on into Advent. For all its nine Sundays there has been no more serious treatment of Advent than before.

The present proposals have been able to learn from that cul-de-sac. They share with the JLG scheme a desire to extend Advent. Yet they do not suggest nine weeks, but seven. They do indicate how to make the season distinctive, and they do remain faithful to Advent themes. More than that, as we have already seen, they integrate Advent with the All Saints'–All Souls' celebration, and so give the calendar for the autumn a new integrity.

The three Sundays between All Saints' Sunday and

Advent Sunday have been designated 'Sundays of the Kingdom'. They are to be given an Advent flavour, the Advent liturgical colour is to be worn, and much of the material in Chapter 4 of *The Promise of His Glory* is suitable for use during these weeks. The proposals have gone as far as possible to make these Sundays of Advent, but have recognized that in terms of the titles given to Sundays the four-week Advent (complete with its wreath nowadays!) is too well established. 'Sundays of the Kingdom' seems to give the right hints, and the titles are backed up with plenty of liturgical material. The Confession, for instance, may be introduced:

> Jesus says, Repent, for the kingdom of heaven is close at hand. So let us turn away from sin and turn to him, confessing our sins in penitence and faith

and one of the Confessions begins,

> Lord Jesus, you came to gather the nations into the peace of your kingdom: Lord, have mercy.

Part of the rationale of these three Sundays is that they are not artificially imposed, but reflect established themes. The first of these three Sundays will be Remembrance Sunday. Reflecting on the Kingdom on Remembrance Sunday will be a natural thing to do, and the lectionary will aid the exercise, whereas combining Remembrance Sunday with Abraham was always something of a nightmare. The third of the Sundays – the 'Stir up' Sunday of the Anglican tradition – is, for those who follow the Roman calendar, The Feast of Christ the King. Here the Commission has tried to use that emphasis but to give it a more Advent, less festal, flavour, reflecting on the kingship of Christ in a way that puts us in mind of his judgement and his salvation. As one of the new eucharistic prefaces for this season expresses it:

> And now we give you thanks because you anointed Jesus Christ, your only Son, as priest and king. Crowned with thorns, he offered his life upon the cross, that he might draw all people into that kingdom where now he reigns in glory.

Mention has been made of the flavour, the distinctive character, of the liturgy in Advent. Advent, we are told, is a bit like Lent, but not altogether so. They certainly do have some things in common. There is, for instance, an element of penitence to Advent. But that, in Advent, is not the principal constituent. First and foremost among the characteristics of Advent is *expectation.* 'Come, Lord Jesus' is a prayer of confidence and of longing, and it is that feeling that must dominate the liturgy through these weeks. Because there is confidence, there is a kind of solemn joy, but because there is penitence there is a restraint as well. Nevertheless it is expectation that gives the season its movement, direction and anticipation. In outward symbol, dark coloured vestments, greenery rather than flowers, the Advent wreath with its candles, can all make the church look like Advent. In the words of worship, more Kyrie than Gloria, a wider use of Old Testament material, canticles with an Advent emphasis, and generous use of the Advent eucharistic material in *The Promise of His Glory* can all contribute.

And what of the anticipation of Christmas? Is it very wicked, as the purists sometimes say? It would be good if we could hold the line through until Advent 2, insisting up to that point that it is a *Second* Coming about which we are reflecting. Thereafter, having given the Advent themes a serious treatment, we do well not to be churlish, not to despise a world that is taking an interest in one of our stories, but to prepare people to celebrate the *First* Coming, so that Christ can be born in them today, so to speak, by telling the story in word and song, but always, as far as we are able, keeping hold of a sense of developing movement towards a climax on Christmas Day. We keep the story unfolding, we keep just some things, whether it be Blessing the Crib, or John 1.1–14, or 'Once in royal David's city', or all three, till Christmas itself, so that the effect is one where everything before 25 December has been preparation, getting ready, rather than simply jumping the gun. It will be easier to do this now that the Church has given us so much rich material to use.

In many churches the first special liturgy before Christmas is a service on Advent Sunday, sometimes called an 'Advent Carol Service'. This term is misleading, and some go away from such a service disappointed, for the word 'carol' made them believe they would sing Christmas songs! It may well be better to call it simply 'The Advent Liturgy'. This is normally an extended word service, reflecting on some of the Scriptures that have an Advent emphasis or that prepare us for Christmas. Chapter 2 has already provided us with sets of such Scriptures and given the opportunity to develop *one* theme systematically instead of taking in a variety of disconnected Old Testament material with a vaguely pre-Christmas feel.

There will tend to be a prejudice in favour of the 'Looking for the Light' set of readings, simply because of the enormous growth of candlelight services. It would be a pity if these readings were always used. The light theme can be honoured by an opening *Lucernare*, but then, in different years, a different Advent theme developed. There has also been a growth of Advent processional services where choir and ministers, if not the whole congregation, move through a great church in a movement symbolic of a journey to find the Christ. The sets of readings in Chapter 2 accord well with such an approach, for there is about a service that builds towards the gospel reading at the end just that sense of development and movement.

The Promise of His Glory provides four sets of opening greeting and introduction for an Advent Liturgy. The first is a general Advent bidding, the second lays emphasis on the 'coming Kingdom' concept, the third introduces an intercessory element (and has resonances with the Milner-White Christmas bidding), and the fourth, which includes the Advent Sunday Collect, develops the light theme.

Although a Service of Light leads very naturally into a first reading at a Vigil Service, the placing of one of these introductions after the kindling of light and before the cycle of readings would not be an intrusion. At the other end of the service, after responsories and prayers, one of the two Solemn Blessings for Advent, both trinitarian in their style, would be appropriate.

Two Penitential Services are also provided for the Advent season. As in *Lent, Holy Week, Easter*, where two such services were also given, here is an attempt to help the Church regain a sense of corporate penitence. Many complain that the new mainstream liturgies are short on penitence, and indeed there had been a clear reaction against the gloom and doom of the past. But now people are asking for occasions to reflect on human frailty and sinfulness. They are not, however, in any traditional sense, flocking to sacramental confession. We need to provide them with services that reflect on our human condition and on the judgement and mercy of a loving God, that give space for thinking, praying and confessing, and that send people away feeling they have made some progress in preparing to keep the coming festival, whichever it may be.

This Advent material is centred around two traditional aspects of the Advent season. The first is the 'Four Last Things': Death, Judgement, Heaven and Hell. The second is the Great Advent Antiphons, made popular by the hymn 'O come, O come, Emmanuel'. These two ways into penitence give the services a quite distinctive Advent flavour, and make them very much services of expectation as much as penitence, and that is true to the spirit of the season.

If they are to fulfil their function as penitential rites, they are in many settings probably not best used as 'The Advent Liturgy', which strikes a slightly different note. Whether on Sunday or weekday, whether with music or not, they are fairly austere acts of worship, probably at their best with little ceremonial, but quite a lot of silence. Hints are given on how they may be combined with Morning or Evening Prayer and with the Eucharist. What is crucial if they are to be Services of Penitence is that they do reach a point where there is space for confession and absolution. They must not be simply reflections on our fragile mortality, but must bring us to our knees and raise us up again. The second of them wisely reminds us:

> The Act of Penitence and Reconciliation has four parts:
>
> Examination of conscience
> Prayer for God's mercy
> Act of Penitence and Contrition
> Declaration of Absolution

Silence and singing may all be part of it, but some structure along these lines is important if people are to come through and go away at peace and with thankfulness.

The Act of Absolution in this rite is a new prayer that may help the Church of England to find a way forward with a formula of absolution that has a strong personal feel to it and yet which expresses the corporate aspect of giving and receiving absolution. The president stands and says, with arms outstretched:

> God, the Father of mercies,
> has reconciled the world to himself,
> through the death and resurrection of his Son Jesus Christ,
> not counting our trespasses, but sending his Holy Spirit
> to shed abroad his love among us.
> By the ministry of reconciliation,
> entrusted by Christ to his Church,
> receive his pardon and peace,
> to stand before him in his strength alone,
> this day and evermore.

These are words that many pastors will find useful quite outside the Advent season and formal services of penitence.

Chapter 4 then provides propers for the period from after The Commemoration of the Faithful Departed through till Christmas Eve, the 'extended Advent' which the calendar envisages. There is no principal Eucharist of the season in the same way as there is for All Saints or for Christmas, and so what is given is not a complete service order for a particular day, but resource material for a whole season. This brings out an important point, that it is the whole season that needs to have an Advent feel, rather than one or two particular liturgies within it, and, on the whole, churches using Holy Communion Rite A have been unimaginative in how they use the freedom to employ 'other suitable words'. Here are a great many other suitable words for use through this season.

The Intercession, with its 'Maranatha', probably needs a word of introduction on the first few occasions that it is used, something to the effect that:

> 'Maranatha' is Aramaic for 'The Lord comes'. It is the note on which the Bible ends in Revelation. In Advent we too pray

'Come, Lord Jesus'.

Unlike some of the other special Intercessions in the book, this one can sustain a certain amount of interpolation of local material, and so may well be a suitable vehicle for intercession quite regularly at the Eucharist through Advent.

The Introductions to the Greeting of Peace are both preferable in Advent to the one provided for that season in the ASB. 'Our Saviour Christ is the Prince of Peace . . .' is better kept for Christmas. The words from the Benedictus are particularly suitable in the week of Advent 3, but are appropriate throughout the season.

The rich collection of prefaces and post-communion collects needs to be used with some sensitivity to the stage the season has reached. Some emphasize the Kingdom, some the prophets, some point to John the Baptist and some to Mary, while others draw these together to express the themes of the season in a unity. A note draws attention to the old tradition of using the Advent Collect daily. Its use after the Collect of the Day would not fit with our renewed understanding of the function of the opening collect, but where people want to retain it throughout the season – and it is a fine prayer – the post-communion slot provides it with a satisfactory home.

This section ends with a number of blessings. The two Solemn Blessings have already been mentioned. The simpler ones that follow are both an improvement on that in the ASB, since both restore the sense of future coming that the ASB text has lost.

The final section of this chapter is entitled 'Church and Home' and treats some popular pre-Christmas observances which might find a place at home as well as in church. The most substantial of them is the tradition of the Advent wreath, now well established in many churches. It is possible to light the five candles (one for each Sunday of Advent and a fifth on Christmas Day) without teaching or prayer that gives each a particular theme. But very often it will seem a fine teaching opportunity not to be missed to help people, especially children, to learn about those who prepared for the coming of Christ, and thus to prepare themselves. There are a number of different schemes that do this. *The Promise of*

His Glory opts for the one that accords best with its lectionary, and this gives us The Patriarchs on Advent 1, the Prophets on Advent 2, John the Baptist on Advent 3, Mary on Advent 4, and Christ himself on Christmas Day.

For each of the five days it gives three prayers. The first prayer in each case conforms to the diaconal blessing of light style associated with a *Lucernare*, and could of course be chanted. 'Blessed are you, Sovereign Lord . . .' they all begin. The second is essentially a teaching prayer, drawing together in a fairly tight form the truths that any little homily at the candle lighting might have expounded. Thus the second prayer for Advent 3 includes the briefest of biographies of John the Baptist:

> God our Father,
> you gave to Zechariah and Elizabeth in their old age
> a son called John.
> He grew up strong in spirit,
> prepared the people for the coming of the Lord,
> and baptized them in the Jordan to wash away their sins:
> Help us, who have been baptized into Christ,
> to be ready to welcome him into our hearts,
> and to grow strong in faith by the power of the Spirit.
> We ask this through Jesus Christ,
> the Light who is coming into the world.

The third set of prayers are simple short-line prayers designed to be said by the whole congregation. They are the sort that could be printed out on a weekly notice sheet or even repeated line by line after the minister.

Because the lighting of the candles of the wreath is partly with children in mind, it will seem appropriate to do this as part of the Sunday service where most of them are present. In the Eucharist, it could be done after the Gospel, or after the Sermon (if the Sermon is linked with the same themes) or after Communion, where one or more of these prayers naturally fill the post-communion prayer slot.

An increasing number of people have an Advent wreath at home. Here is a particular opportunity for a link to be made between church liturgy and home prayers. The third set of wreath prayers, for instance, would be very suitable in homes. And there are other points of contact between church and home at Christmas time. Many families have a crib. Nearly all have a tree, whether it is decorated as a Jesse Tree, as is suggested, or more conventionally. By providing prayers to be said at home at the lighting of candles, at the setting up of a crib, and the lighting up of the tree, the priest helps to strengthen that link, and provides the breakthrough into communal prayers in the home at a time of year when this can be done quite naturally. The hope then is that it will last into other parts of the year, and the chapter ends with material for Saturday night prayers at home that are not particularly restricted to the Advent–Christmas season. By this means Family Prayers, in a new style, might be restored in Christian homes where people have been too self-conscious to attempt it for a while.

FIVE

Christmas

I

Adam lay ybounden, bounden in a bond.
Four thousand winter thought he not too long.
And all was for an apple, an apple that he took,
As clerkes finden, written in the book.
Ne had the apple taken been,
Ne had never Our Lady been a heavene Queen.
Blessed be the time that apple taken was.
Therefore we moun singen *Deo gracias*.

The fourteenth century was a rich time for English literature. It was the century in which the vernacular marriage-vow, now known all over the English-speaking world, was born. It was also the time when this poem was written, now also known throughout the English-speaking community because of its association with the King's College Cambridge Christmas Eve Carol Service.

Adam is the human race, locked tight in sin, because of the apple that he ate, symbolically signalling his independence from God. It was wrong – but it had to happen . . . because if it had not happened, Jesus would not have been sent into the world to put things right. Mary would not have brought him to birth. So it was good that Adam ate the apple, the apple of which we can read, with the help of clerks, in the good 'book'. And Adam in retrospect is so pleased that he was bound for so long in sin, because of the glorious redemption wrought by the holy child. And it does not stop there, for *we* are the ones who benefit. This is no bald theological language, nor archaic poetry. It is a story about life and death, sin and forgiveness, birth and rebirth. Every time we get it wrong, we are able to call upon, claim, plead for the mercy that is to be found beginning at that Christmas crib, and going on through the ministry and work of Christ that never ends for us this side of eternity.

The theological groundplan of that poem dates, of course,

from a much earlier time. Right at the end of the fourth century, a whole thousand years before it was written, Ambrose of Milan reflected on the true significance of Christ's work for us, and a common theme runs through some of his thinking, such as the following:

> My blame has become for me the price of redemption, through which Christ came for me . . . The blame is more fruitful than innocence!
>
> (*Sermon on James 1.21*)

Such a line of thought ultimately produced the 'happy fault' theology, which became embedded in many versions of the Paschal Proclamation over the Easter Candle (the *Exultet*):

> What good would life have been to us,
> had Christ not come as our Redeemer?
> Father, how wonderful your care for us!
> How boundless your merciful love!
> To ransom a slave
> you gave away your Son.
> O happy fault, O necessary sin of Adam,
> which gained for us so great a Redeemer!

Not every local version of the *Exultet* incorporated that powerful utterance – it was not universally popular – and it is optional in many texts today. But it makes the point unmistakably clear that at all levels of Christian thought and experience, what we often call 'incarnation' and 'atonement' belong together. If they are separated, the cash-value of Christianity that ensues becomes hopelessly unbalanced. We often criticize the medievals for lack of balance, sometimes to our own discredit. In Århus Cathedral, Denmark, there is a magnificent late fifteenth-century reredos by Bernt Notke behind the high altar. Like many such works of art from that age, it is able to portray the liturgical year. There is a normal 'ferial'/'festal' array, with great scenes from the lives of saints and figures of the apostles, and the Virgin Mary is being crowned at the very top (or is the crown being removed, in a Lutheran Cathedral?). Then there is an Advent arrangement of the panels, with scenes preparing for the coming of Christ, in which John the Baptist figures prominently. Finally, there is a Lenten arrangement, for which scenes of the passion dominate, and the crowning is concealed from view. But in between the passion panels there is a series of miniatures, depicting Christmas scenes, including the Annunciation and the Visitation. Here in the visual arts is precisely the same doctrinal point being made, with an eloquence unmatched by hectoring homiletics, for the miniatures are situated between the larger panels, and hold them together. Perhaps to make the same sort of impact, but in a different way, there have been several fine hymns written on Adam this century. Pratt Green's version (AMNS 524) picks up Christmas in the third verse in a scene that combines Eden and Bethlehem:

> A little child is Adam's heir,
> is Adam's hope and Lord.
> Sing joyful carols everywhere
> that Eden is restored:
> in Jesus is restored.

Christmas is so familiar to us that it is hard to imagine the Church without it, tempting as that may be on occasion. Historians of liturgy have explained its origins in three ways. First, there is the obvious one, whereby an important gospel event gains its rightful and proper commemoration some time in the fourth century when the rest of the Church Year is reaching its defined state. And that is true. Two of the Gospels (Matthew and Luke) record Jesus' birth. The Fourth Gospel tells of his coming as the 'Word made flesh' (John 1.14). Only Mark omits any reference to the birth; for him, Jesus arrives, first to be baptized and then going into the wilderness, before his preaching and miracles break out. Mark's comparative silence must not be ignored, for it provides an important facet to the greater Christmas season when we come to deal with the meaning of the Epiphany.

The second explanation goes a bit further and takes the line that Christmas (in the West) and Epiphany (in the East) arrived on the scene as a sort of anti-pagan apologetic. According to this theory (which found definitive expression in the works of Bernard Botte and is still referred to as authoritative by such writers as Pierre Jounel) 25 December and 6 January were pagan festivals of the midwinter solstice which had to be christianized, and it was up to the Church to produce a suitable feast in the new religion that would in some sense 'outdo' the old. Thus the festival of the *sol invictus* on 25 December which was popularized at the time of Emperor Marcus Aurelius in 274 should be superseded by the festival of another unconquered sun, the Christ himself. It is an easy theory to explain, but the trouble with it is that there is no hard evidence for 6 January as the solstice festival in the East. Such a 'history of religions' view has been questioned by Thomas Talley (following Duchesne) who has put forward a third explanation, based on calendar calculations. Working on the basis that the rabbis loved to think that important salvific events took place and would take place on the same date, the 'calculation theory' maintains that Christmas and Epiphany were originally chosen in order to occur exactly nine months after the Passover. In the West, the Passover date was taken to be 25 March, and in the East 6 April. Patristic exegesis, never at a loss to explain what was necessary to explain, held that Christ was conceived on the same day as his sufferings and death. In the wake of such associations, we arrive at the two dates, neatly apportioned to the two different parts of the ancient Christian world.

Whichever theory is correct (and the calculation theory has much to commend it, not least in the essential connection that it makes between the two cycles), the fact remains that in the course of the fourth century these two dates emerge in West and East as festivals, of the incarnation, not the nativity. This point is critical to grasp for us who live in an age that sentimentalizes the baby in the crib, with all the commercial trimmings. The same point is made by Cowley:

> In all the ritual of these three Christmas Eucharists there is no emphasis on the infant Lord, but there is indeed high praise to God the Father because the way of salvation has been opened to them who believe by the coming of the divine redeemer. No one can examine these texts and not realize that Christmas is, in origin, a theological feast, a feast of supremely important 'ideas' rather than a 'historical commemoration of an episode'.
>
> (P.Cowley, *Advent – Its Liturgical Significance*, London, Faith Press, 1960, p. 86)

It is, therefore, perhaps a shame that one of the last editorial touches made to the Prayer Book was a series of explications that included altering the plain 'Christmas Day' of the first Prayer Books to the following: 'The Nativity of our Lord, or the Birthday of Christ, commonly called Christmas Day'.

As to history, there is evidence that Christmas was celebrated in Rome by the year 330, though Talley thinks that the Donatists in North Africa commemorated it earlier still. In time, the East took 25 December as an additional festival, except the Armenians, who have only 6 January.

In the Roman rite, there has been a tradition of celebrating three Masses on Christmas Day, and their varying emphases can be discerned by looking at the texts and prayers used. The earliest is the morning Mass, with Hebrews 1.1–12 and John 1.1–14 as the traditional lections, and the Collect, as Patrick Cowley has shown, is about the totality of redemption. Strangely, these are the most abstract of all the Christmas lections. The midnight Eucharist (originally a Mass 'at night', not necessarily exactly at midnight at all, as Jounel has shown) came on the scene a century later, in the 430s. Its lections are Titus 2.11–15 and Luke 2.1–14, a good combination, and with a collect about the holy night being brightened with the true light. Finally, the 'Dawn' Mass, dating from the sixth century, has Titus 3.4–7 and Luke 2.15–20 as equally appropriate Christmas lections, with a collect that refers to the new light of the incarnate Word. The new lectionaries that have appeared in recent years have had no difficulty in quarrying suitable readings from the Old Testament.

We have already alluded to the rich provision of readings for Carol Services and Vigils in Advent, at Christmas, and after. Whichever schemes are used, it is important to note the essential differences between the gospel writers, and the theological priorities which they bring quite openly to the task before them. The distinguished Roman Catholic biblical scholar, Raymond Brown, has done much to set these ideas in context in his great book, *The Birth of the Messiah*. For in Luke's Gospel, the action centres round Mary, and is motivated by angels. Luke, as an outsider by origin, is captivated by the response of old Israel to the revelation, hence the shepherds. Another peculiarity is his interest in liturgical canticles; there are no fewer than four which subsequently appear in the Church's liturgy: the *Benedictus*, the *Magnificat*, the *Gloria in excelsis* (albeit subsequently extended) and the *Nunc Dimittis*. Matthew, on the other hand, has the action motivated by dreams; Joseph takes Mary with him; and being an insider to Judaism Matthew reflects on the response of outsiders to the coming of Christ: hence the Magi. A favourite device is his love of Old Testament prophecy fulfilment. Both Luke and Matthew bring in forebodings of suffering to come, Luke in Simeon's second oracle (we shall discuss this in a wider context in a later chapter), and Matthew more explicitly in the story of the Innocents. The Fourth Gospel, however, goes its own way. The prologue, so very familiar to generations of Christmas worshippers, may well be a later addition (along with the 'Galilean fantasia' in John 21) to the original version. It is the only part of the Gospel in which the term 'Word' is used, but since it is the best-known part, people tend to assume that it is somehow used throughout – which it is not. Most important of all for this Gospel is the word 'glory'. When we hear the words, 'and we beheld his glory', we tend to think of the baby wrapped in swaddling clothes, but for the author of this Gospel the 'glory' is not fully disclosed until the cross.

Liturgists are sometimes accused of ignoring developments in biblical studies. At festivals, this is sometimes a hard warning to heed, so embedded in popular consciousness is the repertoire of Christmas (and Easter) lections. One of the most crucial outcomes of scholarship in recent years is the emphasis placed on the individual author's intentions and priorities. Lectionaries and preaching should reflect this; and that is one reason why (as we shall see in a later chapter) the three-year Roman Lectionary is to be favoured. But when prayers are written it is impossible to be self-consciously 'Marcan' in one prayer, 'Lucan' in another, 'Matthean' in another, and 'Johannine' in yet another. However, in the responsorial Christmas confession, an attempt has been made to paint different pictures from the infancy narratives, and then produce, in the absolution, a Johannine image of beholding the glory of Christ in the cross.

Christmas is normally so full of special services that, when it is all over, it is quite hard to keep going. The contemporary tendency to celebrate by anticipation rather than by actuality makes observing the Christmas saints yet more difficult. But they arrive on the scene for a definite reason, and surprisingly early.

Stephen is mentioned in the fourth-century Syriac Breviary, as is John the Evangelist. Moreover, the fifth-century Armenian Lectionary mentions the commemoration of Stephen at Jerusalem two days after Epiphany (Christmas, as far as we are concerned, in Jerusalem at that time), and also the reading of the slaughter of the Holy Innocents comes the next day. But why?

To commemorate Stephen the day after the celebration of the incarnation makes the point directly that there is a *cost* in following Christ. It is a sobering reminder that martyrdom is a common experience in the Christian religion and Stephen is by tradition the first of these.

To commemorate John the Evangelist on the following day is to make the other point, that not all followers of Christ are called upon to die for their faith, and this particular person is, by tradition, the one who authored the Fourth Gospel, whose spirituality has a prominent place in the lectionaries of all the Churches.

To commemorate the Holy Innocents is to pick up part of the story from one of the Gospel-writers (in this case, Matthew) and to provide an opportunity for remembering unintended martyrs (the 'wordless witness' as the Post-Communion for this day puts it). In the East, the number of the Innocents came to be regarded as 14,000 in all (clearly far in excess of the probable reality), and it was also the day when the Church commemorated victims of famine, thirst, sword, and the cold. All those categories remain and even increase in our own century. In medieval England it was in some places customary to celebrate this day with muffled peals and black vestments. In the provisions for these days, the opportunity has been taken to use Proper Prefaces, although these do not occur in the 1970 Roman Missal (though they *do* appear in the old Sacramentaries). Thus the Preface for Stephen is adapted from the eighth-century Gelasian Sacramentaries, and those for John and the Innocents are inspired by various sources. The Post-Communion Prayers are (for Stephen and John) adapted from the 1970 Missal, where they were from older sources.

II

Chapter 5 of *The Promise of His Glory* is concerned not only with the celebration of the twelve days from Christmas to Epiphany, but also with those services in late Advent that prepare people for the Christmas festival. It is, as has been noted, a difficult time to be innovative, for public taste is at its most conservative at festivals. Yet, for the church and minister where there is a lot of worship at Christmas the need is for variety, for every celebration to have its own character, and for each successive service to move the story on, so to speak, so that there is never a dull sameness, even when there are six Carol Services, a Christingle and a Crib Service all crammed into a week! *The Promise of His Glory* helps.

The chapter opens with provision for the Christmas Carol Service. Time was when the purists would never allow a Christmas Carol Service before 25 December, even though in a number of communities it was all but impossible to get people to come to one after Christmas Day. But, if we have kept a full Advent, stretching back into November, there is no great harm in a Carol Service a few days before Christmas so long as, again, it has the feel of *preparation* about it.

As with Advent, the suggestion is for the use of one of the sets of vigil readings, preceded possibly by a *Lucernare*, with one of the Christmas light blessings, and with a bidding prayer. The traditional King's College Cambridge version is given, and a newer one that first appeared in David Silk's *Prayers for Use at the Alternative Services*.

In many parishes the King's College Cambridge sequence of readings, with perhaps some minor variations, will inevitably win the day, for it is so well established. But those who plan carol services do well to heed the message already given about mixing gospel accounts. Each account has its own integrity, and we confuse rather than enrich the story when we combine them artificially. Not everywhere has this problem, for a traditional and unchanging Carol Service is not established everywhere, and here people will be able to draw much more freely on material, not only in the Service of Light chapter, and in the Carol Service material here, but also in all the provision for Christmas Eve and Day, to create something fresh.

After the Carol Service comes the Christingle Service. It is very easy for the liturgist or the parish priest to be rather dismissive of this service form. In the same way as the Advent wreath, though it may originate with St Lucy's Day in Scandinavia, seems to have come to us from BBC Television's 'Blue Peter' programme, so the Christingle Service, though it may be Moravian in origin, seems to owe more to the good salesmanship of the Children's Society! The service forms that have been in use for the last twenty years leave something to be desired; the hymns written for the service have bordered on the banal. The concept of the Christingle involves some really quite sophisticated explanation. Yet the service has often taken over from the more old-fashioned Crib Service with its excellent teaching that had the power to unfold the Christmas story with appealing simplicity.

For all that, the Christingle Service has established itself quite remarkably, people come in great numbers to it, and are entranced by processions of children winding around the church not quite setting each other alight. And maybe some of the deep truths about Christ, his coming and his salvation for the world get through. So the Church would do well to be positive, to recognize here a liturgical form to which people are attracted, and to ensure that what is provided is the very best.

The form of service given in *The Promise of His Glory* should replace previous ones very quickly, for it is so much better than any of them. Below the surface one can detect the more conventional *Lucernare*, but the blessing of light, or thanksgiving over it, has become congregational and responsorial. Additionally Bishop Timothy Dudley-Smith has written a fine hymn, 'God whose love is everywhere', that succeeds in teaching what the Christingle stands for without declining into doggerel:

> Mark what love the Lord displayed,
> all our sins upon him laid,
> by his blood our ransom paid;
> praise the God of love!
> Circled by that scarlet band,
> all the world is in his hand;
> praise the God of love!

But when should this Christingle Service be held? Provision is made for it to have an Advent, Christmas or Epiphany emphasis. Since it celebrates the light in the darkness, Advent and Epiphany both have claims. There is a further reason for keeping the Christingle Service away from the week before Christmas. It is, quite simply, that in most parishes one cannot sustain a Christingle Service and a Crib Service within a few days of one another. Yet it is the Crib Service that is the better preparation for the Christmas festival. Perhaps best of all is to move the Christingle Service into Epiphany, where the 'light of the nations' and 'Saviour of the whole world' themes can illuminate the Epiphany festival and leave Christmas free for the worship centred on the crib. As long as there are still envelopes for the Children's Society, all will be well!

Section D provides a Crib Service. This is a suggested form for Christmas Eve. It would also be suitable for use on the Fourth Sunday in Advent. It is a simple service, though one that could be built into a longer vigil-type service if that were required. In most parish churches, with a congregation of children, this is unlikely! The service begins with a light theme, and the possibility of candles being lit (another hidden *Lucernare*!), leading into a time of penitence. The responsive confession is one that reappears in the Christmas Eucharist provision. The *Gloria*, with its Christmas association, and the Collect lead into a Ministry of the Word. This will normally be very simple, though the rubric allows for quite a long section of readings from St Luke's Gospel, where this would be appropriate. The address or homily will follow and will usually be a link into the next section which is centred on the Crib.

Providing that the crib is positioned in a suitable place where it can be seen by the congregation, or else that they can all move to it, the service now reaches its heart as the minister uses the figures that are to be placed in the crib to rehearse the Christmas story, with children not only answering his questions, but helping him put ox and ass, angel and manger, Mary and Joseph into the crib, shepherds quite near, and wise men not too far away. If this is to be done thoroughly, carols may be interspersed, often just one or two verses that move the story on. A rubric notes that it is traditional for the figure of the Christ Child to be placed in the crib at the time of the First Eucharist of Christmas. This is not only good liturgy, but good psychology too, for children will have to return on Christmas morning to see the scene complete! And so it is that the words that follow are not a Blessing of the Crib, for that has been made a key element in the Christmas Eucharist rite, but a responsive Thanksgiving at the Crib. In many churches this is an occasion when children bring gifts, often for distribution through charities to children in need. With the crib complete, it makes sense for these gifts to be brought up and left at the foot of the crib, probably while carols are sung. The service ends with Intercession Prayers, which earth the incarnation in the sad realities of this world, and then with the Lord's Prayer and a Blessing.

The major liturgy of Christmas is, of course, the principal Eucharist of Christmas Day, whether celebrated in the middle of the night or in the morning. *The Promise of His Glory* provides a full rite for this occasion, and some of the material within it will also be usable at a second Eucharist on Christmas Day and on the other days before Epiphany.

In terms of structure the most striking feature of the service is the beginning. The Commission has created a kind of fore-rite at the crib and placed there, before ever the president and other ministers approach the altar, both a dedication of the crib and also penitential prayers. The service begins with the ministers, still on their way to the altar, so to speak, coming to the crib (with implications for where the crib is to be placed) for a prayer of dedication and blessing. The president places the figure of the Christ Child in the crib before any words are said. After the Blessing of the Crib, there follows a special form of penitential prayers as ministers and people face the crib. Penitence is an appropriate response to the sight of the crib. For as we gaze at the picture of God's love in sending his Son to be born as one of us and to die for us we are brought to our knees by our sin and by his love. It is not just that at a later point the confession would be an intrusion, but that it is absolutely right at this point in the service and with the crib as its focus.

The ministers then move to 'the place where the Ministry of the Word is celebrated', be that lectern, chair or altar. Where a substantial hymn has already been used on the way to the crib, the song of the angels, *Gloria in excelsis*, may now be sung as the procession completes its journey, but a hymn may be substituted and the *Gloria* saved until after the Greeting. A lot depends both on the musical tradition and the geography of each church.

The Eucharist proceeds with Collect and readings. The Gospel is highlighted on this day by an acclamation to round it off:

Today Christ is born:
Alleluia!
Today the Saviour has come:
Alleluia!
Today the angels sing on earth:
Alleluia! Glory to God in the highest!

The Prayers of Intercession, which allow for only very brief insertions, for they follow a tight construction, are inspired by the *Exultet* of Easter night, with its repeated 'This is the night when . . . .' Here the form is 'In this holy night . . .', with a note indicating a change to 'On this holy day' if used in the morning. There are ten petitions each with this beginning:

Father, in this holy night your Son our Saviour was born in human form: renew your Church as the body of Christ . . .

In this holy night Mary in the pain of labour brought your Son to birth: hold in your hand (. . . and) and all who are in pain or

> distress today. . .
>
> In this holy night heaven is come down to earth, and earth is raised to heaven: keep in safety (. . . and) all those who have gone through death in the hope of heaven . . .

and so on.

There are special words at the Greeting of Peace before the Distribution and at the Post-Communion. The service ends with a threefold Solemn Blessing that has been written around the much loved Milner-White 'May he who by his incarnation . . .' blessing that the ASB includes in a suspect form. Though it is printed only in this rite, it is suitable at all the major liturgies of this season:

> May the Father,
> who has loved the eternal Son
> from before the foundation of the world,
> shed that love upon you his children. **Amen.**
>
> May Christ,
> who by his incarnation gathered into one
> things earthly and heavenly,
> fill you with joy and peace. **Amen.**
>
> May the Holy Spirit,
> by whose overshadowing Mary became the Godbearer,
> give you grace to carry the good news of Christ. **Amen.**

There is a separate service, or at least a series of building blocks to make a separate service, for Christmas morning. In some churches this will form the basis for a non-eucharistic Family Service. In other churches, when there has not been a midnight celebration, this provision will be mainly ignored, because it will be the principal Eucharist of Christmas Day (described above) that will be used. In yet other churches Christmas mid-morning will mean a second Eucharist, but this time one more geared to the young and to families. In this case, a judicious mixture of material from the midnight service and from this additional morning provision will be wise. In churches where the Crib Service material was not used on Christmas Eve, it provides further resources for this morning.

In this morning form there is a new Greeting and Introduction, a different form of both Penitence and Intercession from those in the earlier eucharistic order, a Thanksgiving that could become a eucharistic Preface but could stand on its own, and an alternative form of Creed. This form (which is also authorized though not printed in full in the earlier service) is the appropriate part of the Athanasian Creed, though whether anybody can cope with 'hybrid nature' on Christmas morning remains to be seen!

How to use Christmas morning has become a real problem in some churches where 'everybody' seems to have come at midnight and congregations in the morning are low. In reality, of course, not 'everybody' has come at midnight, and it is particularly sad for the very young and the very old if they come to church on a great festival and find it very much a low day compared with an ordinary Sunday. Making sure that Christmas morning, whether the congregation is large or small, has a festal air and a real sense of joy is an important task for the minister. It may involve not overloading the pre-Christmas programme so that there is nothing new left to unfold on this day. It may mean a form of service, eucharistic or not, that is sufficiently different from an ordinary Sunday that comparisons cannot be made.

In a large church it may mean a procession of children to the crib: 'Christians awake, salute the happy morn' comes marvellously to life with a president processing around the church like a pied piper gathering children as he makes his way to the crib to show them the Christ Child within it and pray with them there. The service will also need to bring in the lighting of the last candle on the wreath with its congregational prayer:

Lord Jesus, Light of Light,
you have come among us.
Help us who live by your light
to shine as light in your world.
Glory to God in the highest.

A word needs to be said about the lections, especially the gospel readings, on Christmas Day. The tradition is to read Luke 2.1–14 at midnight and John 1.1–14 mid-morning, and the lectionary in *The Promise of His Glory* does the same. But this often seems the wrong way round. Midnight has an adult congregation which can relate easily to the John Gospel – light in darkness – whereas the morning congregation has many children who want a story. The note in the lectionary that the readings may be interchanged according to pastoral need should be taken on board. Similarly Hebrews 1 may not go well at the Family Communion, whereas Isaiah 9.2–7 might be ideal if the lighting of the last candle on the Advent wreath were to follow. The lectionary is there to serve, not to be served.

Chapter 4 moves on to provide various prayers for use at the crib. They include the form of blessing already given for the Christmas Day Eucharist. This section anticipates that there will be various occasions of prayer at the crib in the Christmas season. It has already been suggested above that the entrance procession on Christmas Day should go via the crib for a prayer, with the president possibly taking the children with him. A similar 'station' during the opening hymn would be appropriate at the Eucharist each Sunday through Christmas and Epiphany, as would a pause and a prayer at the crib in an Evensong-type procession. This section provides more than adequate material for these occasions.

Additional propers are then given for the three days after Christmas. The ASB already has Collects for St Stephen, St John and the Holy Innocents, and these are not replaced, but Prefaces and Post-Communions are added. They bring together the Christmas truths with the memory of those whom they commemorate so that one is not being pulled in two directions by conflicting themes.

The chapter ends with material for welcoming the New Year. At first the provision may seem small for an occasion that the secular world seems to celebrate with more and more determination. There are some sentences, collects, suggested lections, intercessions and a blessing. But the provision is much richer than at first appears. The Christian Church may be ambivalent about the secular New Year, indeed about new years at all when it prefers cycles of seasons (and cycles have neither beginning nor end), but it has not been ungenerous in what it has provided here. This is partly because there is, in effect, a Watch Night Service, by using the 'Service of Light + Vigil + Readings' formula, and Chapter 2 has included a Blessing of Light for the New Year and a whole set of New Year Vigil Readings. It is also because Chapter 5, in its liturgy for the Epiphany, draws into a renewal of baptismal vows material from the Covenant Service that Methodists have used to usher in the New Year. It is to that chapter, and to the Epiphany, that we now must turn.

SIX

Epiphany

I

> Today the Church has been joined to her heavenly bridegroom, since Christ has purified her of her sins in the river Jordan: the Magi hasten to the royal wedding and offer gifts: the wedding guests rejoice since Christ has changed water into wine, Alleluia.

To the average Christian, these words strike an unfamiliar chord, so habituated are we to view the Epiphany as the commemoration of the story of the three wise men (there were, of course, three, even though the New Testament does not specify the number!). But as we have so far discovered repeatedly in looking afresh at this venerable cycle of Christian feasts and fasts, earlier tradition has a habit of holding different and complementary truths in tension. Nowhere is this paradoxical language more apparent than in the traditional associations with 6 January, the Feast of the Epiphany.

The antiphon quoted earlier is taken from the new Roman Catholic Liturgy of the Hours, which in turn came from the old Roman Breviary. It is appointed before and after the Benedictus canticle at Morning Prayer. Tucked away in the corner of a service that relatively few people will actually use on this day, it forms a sort of relic of an old tradition, that regarded Epiphany as a threefold feast, in which the Marcan narrative of the baptism of Christ is the starting point, leading into the Matthean coming of the Magi to Bethlehem, in turn leading into the Johannine 'sign' of the turning of the water into wine.

Putting these three stories together is, really, exactly what Christians are apt to do on other occasions, namely to draw together seemingly disparate sections of Scripture and from them form some sort of unified whole. And that is what the three associations of Epiphany do. They represent a way of keeping the mystery of the incarnation together at a time when it is in danger of being romanticized. It has a good pedigree, as we shall see. It seeks to make plain that we are NOT celebrating Christmas in order to coo over babies, but rather to celebrate the start of Christ's ministry, a ministry that from the very beginning held within it all the features that were to mark its ending – and rebirth, after the resurrection. It is for this reason that it is a shame that, yet again, the 1662 Prayer Book should have added the narrowing definition of Epiphany as 'The Manifestation of Christ to the Gentiles'. (Lutherans call it 'Holy Three Kings', pictorial but limiting.) Manifestation it definitely is, but perhaps Christopher Wordsworth captured the full meaning of the manifestations in terms far wider than most worshippers (clergy included) think today:

Songs of thankfulness and praise,
Jesu, Lord, to thee we raise,
manifested by the star
to the sages from afar;
branch of royal David's stem
in thy birth at Bethlehem:
anthems be to thee addrest,
God in Man made manifest.

Manifest at Jordan's stream,
Prophet, Priest, and King supreme;
and at Cana wedding-guest
in thy godhead manifest;
manifest in power divine,
changing water into wine:
anthems be to thee addrest,
God in Man made manifest.

Two verses follow on the ministry of Christ and the Second Coming. The final verse sums it all up:

Grant us grace to see thee, Lord,
mirrored in thy holy word;
may we imitate thee now,
and be pure, as pure art thou;
that we like to thee may be
at thy great Epiphany;
and may praise thee, ever blest,
God in Man made manifest.

Epiphany, then, is more than wise men coming from the East, it is a rounded festival of the disclosure of God's glory, and it is all the more necessary to link these three traditional themes together at a time when the whole Christmas cycle is under pressure of trivialization. It is timely that the truly radical and traditional view of worship as *theophany* (the title for the feast in the Byzantine rite) should be brought out of the Church's cupboard and given its true place as the centre of a new and more dynamic approach to what we do in church. In an age that still tends to worship 'relevance', it is perhaps appropriate to remember some words of Aidan Kavanagh, 'Nothing is so relevant as knowledge, nothing so irrelevant as ignorance.' 'Theophany' has the relevant meaning 'appearance of God'.

As we saw in the previous chapter, three theories attempt to supply the answer to the question, 'Why Christmas and Epiphany?' Epiphany came onto the arena of church history in the fourth century, as part of that trend towards bringing the 'events' of the gospel into special focus. While some scholars think that the midwinter solstice was christianized, there is a growing acceptance that 6 January owes its origin to being exactly nine months after 6 April, the date which Eastern Christians took to have been the Passover and the day on which Christ was conceived. Egeria's travel diary has 6 January as Epiphany. Unfortunately, the start of her narrative for this day has been lost, but we have enough to go on. She manages to communicate what it felt like to have been there:

> Just after seven in the morning, when the people have rested, they all assemble in the Great Church on Golgotha. And on this day in this church, and at the Anastasis and the Cross and Bethlehem, the decorations really are too marvellous for words. All you can see is gold and jewels and silk; the hangings are entirely silk with gold stripes, the curtains the same, and everything they use for services at the festival is made of gold and jewels. You simply cannot imagine the number, and the sheer weight of the candles and the tapers and lamps and everything else they use for the services.
>
> They are beyond description, and so is the magnificent building itself. (J.Wilkinson, *Egeria's Travels to the Holy Land*, p. 127)

Not only is it all magnificent – it goes on and on, in Bethlehem, for eight days (i.e. an octave). The importance of this festival clearly struck Egeria as of vital importance. In the following century, the old Armenian Lectionary that often illuminates and corresponds with Egeria's account shows a definite preference for the Matthean narrative, interrupting it on the day of St Stephen with John 12.24–6 (the grain of wheat dying). It is clear, however, from both these sources, that Epiphany is a festival of incarnation. But there is at this time, too, the growing additional association of Epiphany with the baptism of Christ, not at Jerusalem, but in Alexandria (which was to show a preference for the Marcan narrative anyway) and in Syria. John Chrysostom preached a sermon at Epiphany in the year 387 which contained the following revealing words:

> For this is the day on which he was baptised and sanctified the nature of the waters. Therefore also on this solemnity in the middle of the night all who are gathered, having drawn the water, set the liquid aside in their houses and preserve it throughout the year, for today the waters are sanctified. And this evident marvel is produced, that this water is not corrupted by the long passage of time, but through an entire year or even two or three years the water drawn today remains pure and fresh, and after such a long time it rivals that just drawn from the spring.

Here is evidence for Epiphany as the feast, above all, of Christ's incarnation through his baptism, surely not a piece of liturgy for the sake of it, but to do with the christological importance of the occasion. Christ sanctified water by being baptized in it, which means that water which is blessed on this day in some special way commemorates the baptism of Jesus. In a hot climate, and one in which the availability of water depended on the weather and season (especially Egypt), such a sanctification of water was an easy development. But it has as much to say to our own world-view today, in which half the population of this planet has easy access to fresh water, while the other half has grave difficulty. Western Christians may live in comfort, but the rise of modern communications, together with the advance of Development

Studies, means that we are both comfortable in ourselves and aware of thirst and deprivation among others. Moreover, we tend to forget that Christ was baptized at the beginning of his ministry, just as most Christians are today. The modern trend to wait until we are all ready before anything happens is a most un-biblical attitude. Baptism, whether ours or Christ's, *leads into* discipleship, is not the summation of it.

Epiphany moved West to Spain and France in the later fourth century and it is in the writings of Maximus of Turin at the end of that century and the start of the following that we come across allusions to the Cana motif at Epiphany. Strangely, there was yet another combination, for Filastrius of Brescia links Magi, baptism, and *transfiguration* together, but we do not come across that again, although the christological significance of the latter is obvious, if not also ingenious. In a century that was hotly debating the incarnation and the Trinity, it became a priority to draw out of the Bible and the worship of the Church a coherent approach to the main tenets of belief. The three associations that are contained in the Roman antiphon quoted earlier first come together, then, in north Italy and southern France in the late fourth and fifth centuries. Magi, baptism, and Cana bring together three important christological themes from the start of three of the Gospels. And it is no coincidence that Epiphany both in France and Spain, and also in the East, becomes one of the occasions for baptism to be celebrated publicly. In the Byzantine rite to this day, there is a special Blessing of the Waters at baptism which is an adaptation of the corresponding blessing of the water at Easter. That provision would not have been made without very good reason, and the reason in this case is the great significance attached to Epiphany baptism. Writing of the three associations, Talley has this to say:

> This multiple theme and the liturgical poetry it inspired carried forward much of the tradition regarding the close interplay between the incarnation, the baptism and the first miracle represented already by the first two chapters of the fourth gospel.

The new services provide a considerable amount of material

and it may even seem at first sight to be rather daunting in scale. Inspired both by the traditions that we have just looked at and by the need to articulate a richer theology and practice of baptism in our own day, there is thus something for everybody. It is not intended to be a sort of esoteric dustbin for those who, in the immortal words of Miss Jean Brodie, 'like that sort of thing'. The 1970 Roman Missal makes the First Sunday after Epiphany the Feast of the Baptism of Christ, and it is possible to keep Epiphany on the Sunday or weekday on which 6 January happens to fall, and then to celebrate the baptism of Christ on the Sunday after. The service for the Epiphany itself can also be celebrated on the Sunday after, and it can be combined with a Eucharist or not, as the case may be. In genre, it is really a 'Cathedral' or 'People's' Office, with a rich use of symbolism, movement, Bible and song. The 'three wonders', as the introduction terms them, appear in the order in which they fit best at a non-eucharistic service, so that Magi lead into Cana, which in turn leads into baptism, and the baptismal liturgy can either include a baptism itself or else take the form of a renewal of the baptismal covenant. (This latter contains as one of its options the Methodist Covenant Renewal, traditionally used at the New Year, in an adapted form.) Alternatively, Cana can come last and lead naturally into the Eucharist, thus forming a somewhat novel structure for the Ministry of the Word at the Eucharist on this occasion.

Much is made of the water, and the suggestion of pouring the water out at the door of the church is an adapted version of Eastern practice on this day. The symbolism is exactly that of the incarnation . . . that the sacred takes over the secular, that the divine and the human mix freely, and that the Church blesses the world, and by so doing ceases from being the holy ghetto that is one of its temptations in our own time.

We have said much of baptism. One final theological aspect that needs emphasizing today is that the link between Epiphany and baptism may well bring out the pneumatological dimension (i.e. teaching about the Holy Spirit) rather more than is possible or even appropriate at Easter. We are in danger of allowing certain sections of the Church to indulge in a sort of secondary theological picketing at the gates of the Holy Spirit. This is a potentially dangerous situation to face, since the connection between baptism and Holy Spirit has always been close at those points in the history of the Church when its sacramental life has been at its healthiest. Today, we have just lived through an unprecedented era of eucharistic renewal and it would seem that we are on the verge of doing the same with baptism. But we can only do it if we keep sacramental faith and practice in some sort of creative tension – and that does *not* mean by keeping them apart. Too many people in the Western Churches regard their baptism as a kind of *anamnesis* of Christ's baptism, and not as an *epiclesis* of the Spirit in the future. Epiphany, which in so many other respects is an occasion of promise for the future, provides exactly the right context for renewing not the sacrament itself so much as the perspectives we bring to it. We are in danger of over-packaging Christian experience and of defining how God is supposed to act. It is a very cerebral approach, often backed up by well-intentioned thoughts from the Bible. But it is really very alien to the spirit of the New Testament. Epiphany provides a unique opportunity to start again. The new services are intended to do just that – and they need to be entered into with courage, vision, and a sense of enjoyment of God's presence and power, not least in those time-honoured and biblical symbols.

In the little antiphon quoted earlier are to be found the words, 'Today the Church *has been joined* to her heavenly bridegroom.' Marriage imagery lies at the heart of many of the hymns, prayers and chants through the Advent–Candlemas season. In the hymn, 'Sleepers wake', we are called upon to be ready to meet the bridegroom. At Candlemas, there is an old Byzantine chant that speaks of 'adorning the bridal chamber'. Here, at Epiphany, the incarnation is seen depicted in a marriage between Christ and his Church (Ephesians 5.23ff.). A quaint outmoded image? Ironically, the very age which is seeing the sacrament of matrimony under more stress than perhaps ever before tends to handle marriage imagery in the New Testament with carefully-balanced tongs, as if it were too hot and tricky to handle. Not for a moment are we suggesting that everything ancient is good and right for today's Church. But it is something of a pity that we tend to ignore it, and there are even exegetes who are determined to iron out of the miracle at Cana any suggestion that it has to do with marriage at all!

Marriage is about union, companionship and procreation, and it is precisely because of these three reasons, enumerated so lovingly by Christian writers down the ages, that the image of Christ marrying the Church for unity, community and future offspring is so deeply traditional and startlingly contemporary. One could almost say that the 'three wonders' of the old Western Epiphany festival correspond to those three reasons; baptism is the union of Christ and his people, the Magi adoring Christ are the community that Christ gathers round him, and Cana holds out promise of a Church of the future, renewed and transformed all the time. It is these depths of reality that the Church is called upon to plumb and be nourished by at such a solemn season.

II

Epiphany is both a feast and a season. The rationale of keeping the spirit of Christmas and Epiphany prominent in the liturgy right through until the Presentation of Christ, Candlemas, on 2 February, will be discussed in the following chapter. But it is important, at this stage, to understand that Epiphany is not seen in this book as the end of Christmas, but as a building on of new layers of incarnation truth to be celebrated through the weeks of January. And here it may be useful to note that the calendar speaks of the Sundays 'of' Epiphany, rather than 'after', to help make that point.

The Promise of His Glory does not insist on this long Epiphany season until Candlemas. It allows for the possibility of returning to green 'ordinary time' once the Baptism of the Lord has been celebrated, and provides in the lectionary for the development of quite other neutral themes through January. Nevertheless the clear logic of the book is a high profile Epiphany season until the forty days from Christmas are complete. This is in contrast to present Roman practice, which reverts to ordinary time once the Baptism is over and leaves Candlemas marooned in a sea of green, with its rationale almost lost. It is difficult to believe that the next round of Roman revision will not follow the same path as *The Promise* in restoring the forty-day incarnation season. It is also a development beyond the ASB. That book half took on board the idea of a season *of*, rather than *after*, Epiphany, providing lectionary themes that develop the idea of Christ's revelation and also an Epiphany Preface right through, yet, as with the period before Advent, it was half-hearted in its reform, and ended up sending out only confusing signals. *The Promise of His Glory* is not confusing. Its clearly preferred route to Candlemas is a full-blooded white festival season, celebrating the revelation of Christ's glory, with an unmistakable change of gear on 3 February.

The three major strands of Epiphany celebration have already been spelt out: the coming of the kings, the baptism in the Jordan, and the water into wine at the wedding feast. *The Promise* sets out to help congregations to regain this threefold truth, and to hold the themes together. The Christian year is nearly always more subtle than people imagine. Perhaps the most important aim for this season has to be to recover the significance of the Lord's baptism. And yet people will not want to do that at the expense of the mainstream expectation about Epiphany, the arrival of the Magi from the East.

The calendar expresses a preference for The Feast of the Epiphany to be kept on 6 January, whatever day of the week that is. This is rather contrary to the line it takes on, for instance, All Saints' Day and The Presentation, both of which it encourages to be given Sunday observance. The reluctance to move the Epiphany to the Sunday arises from two concerns. The first is to ensure that the Baptism of the Lord gets the prominence it deserves, and for that to be the Christian mystery with which people are confronted on the first Sunday of the Epiphany season. The second is a more general desire not to lose the experience of worship in a setting other than that of Sunday mid-morning. Pastorally one cannot fail to see the attractiveness of slotting everything into the Sunday morning pattern, because, in most communities, that is when the greatest number of people will come. But there is no doubt that something is lost. Especially in winter, there are festivals that have a 'light in the darkness' theme to them that conveys itself less powerfully in broad daylight. In an ideal world one would keep All Saints' Day, the Epiphany and Candlemas on their traditional dates with an evening celebration. Looking at it practically, this will not always be the best way to give them prominence. But Epiphany, and the related idea of Twelfth Night, has a stronger place in people's consciousness than many of the other feasts, so there is some chance of building up a worthwhile weekday festival on 6 January. It is worth working at.

Nevertheless, although *The Promise* urges the keeping of the Epiphany on 6 January, it does, for pastoral reasons, allow its transfer to a Sunday between 5 and 12 January. But, when this happens, The Baptism of the Lord is to be moved to the Second Sunday of Epiphany, and the usual lectionary provision for the Second Sunday lost. It is also intended that The Baptism should be the *name* given to a major feast day, not just the *theme* given to something called a 'Sunday of Epiphany'. The Baptism takes its place, with The Presentation, The Transfiguration, and so on, as festivals of Our Lord.

The chapter begins with further material for Vigil Services and with provision for Epiphany Carols. The material that is to follow, in Section C, provides such a strong service shape that it will almost inevitably commend itself to those parishes that try to have one special non-eucharistic service for Epiphany. But other forms are here.

Section C provides the major service for this season. From its opening acclamations it seeks to present and hold together the three strands of the Epiphany celebration:

> Three wonders mark this holy day, as the Church is joined to her heavenly Bridegroom.
>
> This day a star leads the wise men to the manger.
> **Alleluia!**
>
> This day water is made wine at the wedding feast.
> **Alleluia!**

This day Jesus is revealed as the Christ in the waters of baptism.
Alleluia!

Because it is a service that presents this cluster of ideas so effectively, it deserves to be used at the time when its impact can be greatest. The notes indicate that the Feast of the Baptism, the First Sunday of Epiphany, is the best day. Used on that day, it can become the Eucharist of the day, with a three-stage Ministry of the Word leading to communion. Or it can be a non-eucharistic service with baptism and the renewal of baptismal vows as the climax around the font. But it can be used also on the Feast of the Epiphany itself, though, when that happens, a note indicates that the full Matthew 2.1–12 Gospel should be read, rather than the shorter one indicated in the text of the service.

The service will be at its most effective where there is space for the whole congregation to move from one focus to another. There are churches where this is inappropriate, but there are many more where the building is of such a size and layout that it seems tailor-made for such movement. Ideal for this service is a focus for the crib, placed well away from the altar and the font – and not necessarily where it has to stand through the rest of the season – with a space of its own, as well as the more usual focus at the font and at the altar. Ideally the people move to each in turn. Where this is not possible, the ministers go to each and the people turn to face them.

As it stands the service betrays its cathedral origins and could be a little too 'grand' in some parochial settings. This can be resolved by the music. Some of the Christmas carols, especially those with an Epiphany feel, can lighten the service just sufficiently to make its meaning more accessible to ordinary congregations, and the Epiphany hymns themselves enrich it too. Mention has already been made of Bishop Wordsworth's 'Songs of thankfulness and praise', and there is also the fifth-century office hymn of the day ('Why, impious Herod, shouldst thou fear?' or 'How vain the cruel Herod's fear') that treats in turn the three strands of the festival:

Lo, sages from the East are gone
To where the light hath newly shone:
Led on by light to Light they press,
And by their gifts their God confess.

The Lamb of God is manifest
Again in Jordan's water blest,
And he who sin had never known
By washing hath our sins undone.

Yet he that ruleth everything
Can change the nature of the spring,
And gives at Cana this for sign –
The water reddens into wine.

A particular feature of the service is the series of acclamations that greet the bringing in of appropriate symbols. In the first section, that celebrates the coming of the Magi, the symbols are the traditional gifts, gold, incense and myrrh, or, a note explains, just one of those three gifts, placed at the crib, where the Gospel is read. In some communities the use of incense at this point will be entirely appropriate. In others it would be unacceptable. Here simply the gift of gold might be given, and 'gold' here might well mean the congregation's genuine gift of money in the service of Christ. Or else, at this point, while the crib is the focus, the acclamation might be used to greet the crib figures of the kings before they were placed in the crib.

The flagons of water and of wine in the next two sections are more straightforward symbols. The water is poured into the font. Where the context is the Eucharist, the wine may be poured into a chalice on the altar and used for the celebration.

The possibility of Baptism (and Confirmation) at the font as part of this Epiphany rite presents a different angle on Christian initiation. As has already been said, it allows us to see the significance of baptism outside the Easter context that has been particularly fashionable during the last decades of liturgical reform. This is partly to balance the theological emphasis on baptism as an entering into the death and resurrection experience of Christ by affirming the role of the Spirit in Christian baptism, as in the baptism of Christ himself. But, in a wider sense, it is also to place baptism within a season of the incarnation, where all the language of birth and rebirth can be heard in a slightly different way.

It is altogether good that Christians should be moving towards a view that there are particularly appropriate seasons for baptism, and that it is not something for which one day is as helpful as another. But it would be too restricting if only the season from Easter to Pentecost were deemed suitable, and this service encourages new thinking about the suitability of Epiphany as a baptismal season, and this is much to be welcomed, not just by those who will use precisely this rite, but by all those whose theology of baptism will be enriched in seeing how it fits into the Epiphany context.

In its original report form, *The Promise of His Glory* includes an alternative form of this Epiphany service, providing new texts for baptism and confirmation with an Epiphany flavour. Unfortunately, this has had to be omitted from the edition commended for liturgical use, simply because it needs synodical approval before it can be used with authority.

Among the texts of the baptismal rite, there was material that people would do well to consider for use at other times. Five features in particular may be noted:

The Prayer over the Water, which is always much more than simply a Water Blessing, was in a responsorial form that gave more opportunity for tightly packed theological ideas to be assimilated than the ASB Prayer over the Water. Fortunately this is also reproduced in the Thanksgiving section of *Patterns for Worship*.

The Profession of Faith was welcome for returning to an older tradition of using the Apostles' Creed, with its baptismal origin, as the response to the president's questions. That provides a richer form than the terse questions of the ASB rite.

Where confirmation is administered, words were given for the president to use if the candidates were anointed with chrism.

> N, God has called you by name and made you his own.

This is helpful for all confirmations, since at present the ASB provision allows for the use of oil of chrism, but provides no words to accompany its use.

The provision, after baptism and confirmation, for the offering of prayer, and the words addressed to the candidates,

> You now share, with all the members of the Church, the privilege of praying to our Father, through his anointed Son Jesus our Lord, in the power of his Holy Spirit

not only ensured that intercessory prayer formed part of this rite, but also raised the question of whether baptism should not always lead into intercessory prayer, however brief, and that parishes should seek to restore this whenever baptism is celebrated. (One of the Eucharistic Prayers in *Patterns for Worship* restores the intercessory element within that prayer on occasions when it may, because of baptism, be lost at an earlier point in the service.)

The final detailed point from the initiation provision was the moving of the Giving of Light from the immediate post-baptismal ceremonies to the end of the rite, so that it might be seen more clearly that the newly baptized go out *into the world* reflecting the light of Christ. This is clearly preferable to usual practice where a light is given and soon blown out so that the service may move on to something else!

After this major rite, the chapter moves on to sets of material for use at points within the Epiphany season. In Section D provision is made for the Feast of the Epiphany itself, for the Baptism of Christ, and for the rest of the season.

For the Feast of the Epiphany, what is provided is for churches that do not celebrate the major liturgy described above on 6 January, but keep that for later, and so need material to enrich the Feast of the Epiphany itself. What is given is not a complete rite, but material for use at all the variable points in the Eucharist. The most striking inclusion is for the Gospel, which it is suggested should be read at the crib, and acclamations are provided to be used as the gifts are placed there (or as the crib figures are put in). A Solemn

Blessing for the day is provided, but the use of the Solemn Blessing from the earlier rite, picking up on the three strands of Epiphany celebration and bringing them into a trinitarian shape, would ensure that the wider Epiphany significance was not lost even on this day of the kings.

> May God the Father, who led the wise men by the shining of a star to find the Christ, the Light from Light, lead you also in your pilgrimage to find the Lord. **Amen**.
>
> May God the Son, who turned water into wine at the Wedding Feast at Cana, transform your lives and make glad your hearts. **Amen**.
>
> May God the Holy Spirit, who came upon the beloved Son at his baptism in the river Jordan, pour out his gifts on you who have come to the waters of new birth. **Amen**.

The propers for the Baptism of the Lord are provided for the Eucharist on that day, whether it be a conventional straightforward celebration, or whether it be the principal liturgy described above put within a eucharistic context.

The material that follows is for use between 7 January and 2 February. It enables the season to retain its distinctive feel, though it must be added that, as far as sung services are concerned, this will only be achieved if the choice of music, and particularly of hymnody, is also sensitive to the principle that we are still celebrating the incarnation and the glory revealed in the early stories of Christ's life and ministry.

Whereas much of this material will change from day to day, as different choices are made, one little text deserves more regular use through the whole forty days although it is set out in the provision for the Candlemas Eucharist. It is a text, taken over from the Canadian *Book of Alternative Services*, for the breaking of bread, that, for all its simplicity, has a memorable rhythm and gets very near to the heart of what we are celebrating at this season:

> We break the bread of life,
> and that life is the light of the world:
> **God here among us,**
> **light in the midst of us,**
> **bring us to light and life.**

The chapter ends with provision for the two themes of Mission and Unity. The relationship between Epiphany and the Mission of the Church is a clear one and, though we might regret the Book of Common Prayer's rather narrow definition of Epiphany as 'The Manifestation of Christ to the Gentiles', we need to keep before us the call to share very widely the revelation of Christ's light and glory. It is good that *The Promise* will provide the Church with new material to pray about its mission just as the Decade of Evangelism is being launched. This material also, of course, ties up with the Feast of the Conversion of St Paul, the great missionary of early Christianity, and some of it is as likely to prove useful around that feast day (25 January) as earlier in the season.

The unity material is, of course, a response to the Week of Prayer for Christian Unity from 18 to 25 January. No complete service is provided, since, in this of all weeks, services need to be devised ecumenically, and each year has its own emphasis. But there is useful supplementary material here, and, like the material for Baptism and for Mission, its use need not be restricted to January and the Epiphany, but can enrich worship throughout the year.

Nevertheless, at the end of January we have not quite left behind the Christmas and Epiphany truths. They reach their proper end, and a new beginning is made, in the Presentation of Christ in the Temple, of which the next chapter speaks.

SEVEN

Candlemas

I

Hail, O Theotokos Virgin full of grace:
for from thee has shone forth the Sun of righteousness,
Christ our God, giving light to those in darkness.
Be glad also, thou righteous Elder,
for thou hast received in thine arms
the Deliverer of our souls,
who bestows on us the resurrection.

This chant is the Troparion for the feast of 'The Meeting of our Lord', as it is called in the Byzantine rite. Like so many of the Eastern chants, it serves to invoke a scene, rather like the chorus in a Greek tragedy; and it picks out certain individuals within the whole drama: in this case the Virgin Mary, and then Simeon.

It is indeed a rich scene. It comes down to us in only one version – Luke's Gospel. And it is full of ambiguities, as the various titles given to it in liturgical calendars show. The East tends to call it *Hypapante* ('meeting'), stressing the theme of encounter. The Gelasian books refer to it as the feast of the 'Purification', thus making it a feast of the Virgin Mary. The earlier Gregorian books (i.e. 'pure' Roman) call it 'St Simeon', and subtitle it with the Greek *Hypapante*. Some ancient and nearly all modern books call it the 'Presentation', thus grouping it with the feasts of our Lord. But as is so often the case with ambiguity, there is a bit of truth in all of them. It is about 'meeting', but it is a very special meeting, and not only Mary and Simeon are there, but Joseph and Anna. It is about 'purification', but not just the purification of Mary after childbirth; the wider purification is about judgement, and the chilling message of Simeon's second oracle, that a sword pierces through the hearts of those who would follow Christ. It is about Simeon, but also Anna, two elderly people awaiting the Lord's coming. And it is about 'presentation', of ourselves with the Lord, both now and at the end of time. But since this feast is one of those which tends to be undervalued, it is worth looking at the gospel narrative itself in more detail.

The narrative is part of Luke's own sequence of thought, which began with John the Baptist's birth, continued with the annunciation to Mary, and reached its climax in the birth of Christ. In this Temple drama, Luke himself conflates the purification of Mary after childbirth (something necessary for every mother, hence the offering of the turtle-dove or pigeon) and the presentation of the first-born son; such presentation (more accurately 'redemption') involved no sacrifice, but payment of a few shekels. A similar conflation runs through some later Christian rites in both East and West over the question of what to do after childbirth. Some stress 'presentation' of the child, whereas others place the emphasis on 'purification' of the mother. Some even direct the service to take place on the fortieth day after the birth, and may include the reading of part of the Candlemas Gospel, with the *Nunc Dimittis*. Perhaps Luke straddles both themes deliberately, as does the Prayer Book in a somewhat different context when it describes the service as 'The thanksgiving of women after childbirth, commonly called the Churching of Women'. Luke's recurring message, that the Gospel is for women, children, outcasts, and not just for men, and that this Gospel does not make special requirements except faith, obviously keeps having to be made, and keeps having to refashion and prune traditional rites, with their unfortunate overtones of women being unclean.

There are subtleties about this Gospel in the text itself as well as in the traditions which it has inspired. In contrast to John the Baptist, who has only Zechariah to proclaim his birth, Jesus has angels, then Simeon. The angels proclaim Christ as the expectation of Israel, whereas Simeon speaks of Christ fulfilling his destiny 'in the presence of all peoples' (Luke 2.31). The balance of the devout parents with their child is matched by two aged people, who typify Jewish Christian *Anawim*, the poor ones, the pious ones, totally dependent upon God, seeing in Christ their deliverance. The Temple is central to Luke's whole narrative, for it is there that Zechariah is told about the coming birth of his son, and there, too, that the twelve-year old Jesus is taken, lost (supposedly), and found. Raymond Brown waxes eloquent about this particular drama: 'The Law, the prophetic Spirit, and the Temple cult have all come together to set the scene for the greatness of Jesus. The one who is called "holy" (Luke 1.35) has come to the holy place of Israel and he begins to embody much of what was associated with the Temple.' But the contrasts continue. Simeon is looking for the 'consolation' of Israel (Luke 2.25) whereas Anna speaks of the 'redemption' Christ will bring (Luke 2.38). Both Simeon's oracles and the warning to Mary rely on Isaiah's combination of consolation (Isa. 40.1; 66.12–13) and redemption (Isa. 2.38). Simeon's dual role of watchman and aged one combine with the dual emotions of joy and peace.

It could be that, like the inclusion of the *Nunc Dimittis* in the liturgy of Candlemas, the canticle does not really belong to the original recension of this part of the Gospel. But the second oracle poses exegetical questions wrestled with by subsequent ages. When Simeon foretells that a sword will pierce Mary's own soul, he is bringing into the orbit of birth narrative the chilling side of the entire gospel. Mary is the first to hear of the good news of Jesus, and so is also the first to encounter its challenge and the tragedy of its rejection by many in Israel. And Luke, ambivalent about suffocating family loyalties, is perhaps saying that being related to Jesus is not enough. The passage ends with the statement that Jesus 'grew and became strong, filled with wisdom; and the favour of God was upon him' (Luke 2.40), whereas John the Baptist was only 'strong in spirit'. Jesus already has the Spirit.

Luke's narrative, then, is full of different nuances, ones which are impossible to package into a neat compartment. Is the scene a feast of Mary, Jesus, or Simeon? It is really all three, though perhaps we may indicate a preference for 'presentation of the Lord' at this stage. Then, where does the scene belong, in terms of the Church's Year? Luke places it firmly on the fortieth day after birth. (The Byzantine rite has prayers for the fortieth day after birth that allude to Christ's presentation in the Temple.) On the other hand, the Christ depicted by Luke is always a figure who identifies with the forgotten elements of society (here, an old man and a woman, too), which arouse conflict from the start. The chilling second oracle of Simeon brings in the theme of conflict. And that, surely, means that the feast, though joyful in tone, has an underlying feeling of pain and conflict.

So much for the biblical background. What of the feast as a feast? Egeria has this to say about its observance in Jerusalem, clearly a new experience for her:

> Note that the Fortieth Day after Epiphany is observed with special significance. On this day they assemble in the Anastasis. Everyone gathers, and things are done with the same solemnity as at the feast of Easter. All the presbyters preach first, then the bishop, and they interpret the passage from the Gospel about Joseph and Mary taking the Lord to the Temple, and about Simeon and the prophetess Anna, daughter of Phanuel, seeing the Lord, and what they said to him, and about the sacrifice offered by his parents. When all the rest has been done in the proper way, they celebrate the sacrament and have their dismissal. (J. Wilkinson, *Egeria's Travels in the Holy Land*, p. 128)

There is much here. Egeria is struck by the solemnity given to the feast, and the fact that all the presbyters preach, and the Gospel of the day (as we now know it) is read in full. (There is a regrettable tendency in the later West to omit the part referring to Anna.) She also mentions the sacrifice offered – this was a popular theme in patristic exegesis. But we have as yet no mention of the candles which are to dominate Western observance of the feast, and which were to give it the medieval nickname, 'Candlemas'. About seventy years later (*c.* 450) we read of the introduction of candles on this occasion near Jerusalem, which may mean that it was already practised in Jerusalem itself. But it must be noted that we are definitely in the orbit of that part of the Church which celebrates the incarnation on 6 January, so this festival is on 14 February. In the sixth century it was being celebrated in Constantinople.

The gradual appearance of the feast in the West is a confused and confusing picture. At first, it appears to have been observed as part of the octave of Christmas. Then Sergius I (687–701) added it to his list of festivals of the Virgin

Mary that should have a procession. The Gregorian Sacramentary texts provide not just mass-prayers for the occasion, but also a *collecta*, in other words a prayer to be said when everyone has gathered (with candles, in this case) before marching off in procession to the church where the Eucharist is to be celebrated. Such a pre-dawn procession seems to have been a novelty, adding atmosphere to the occasion. The next stage comes in the ninth century when special candle-blessings begin to appear in local service-books. Not all of them, as it happens, actually *bless* the candles. Interestingly, there is a prayer that appears among the assorted additions to the Sacramentary of St Martin's Abbey of Tours (the one which Alcuin of York ruled as abbot for the remaining years of his life after leaving imperial service): it refrains from blessing the candles, and only prays in general terms that the lights may brighten up the temple, so that we may enter the glory of eternal light. This prayer is one of the two texts used for the 1970 Missal at this point. It is also the source, in a more authentic form, of the corresponding prayer over the candles in the eucharistic rite contained in the new book for this occasion.

Having added the *blessing* of candles, the next stage for the medievals was to make complex provision for further blessing (some books have as many as *seven* prayers) and for the distribution of the candles after blessing and then for the chants to be sung during the procession. Among the texts found for the procession is the Troparion quoted at the start of this chapter, and other Byzantine chants were incorporated into the Latin rite for this day, as well. Surprisingly, the *Nunc Dimittis*, which in retrospect seems an obvious winner for this day, has to wait until the twelfth century before being included.

We have already alluded to the trend in many Western lectionaries to omit Anna from the Gospel for this day. Another anomaly concerns the liturgical colour. There was no proper delineation of colour in the West until the thirteenth century, though there were efforts before then to produce some sort of general approach which tended to mean that the elaborate vestments that a church possessed would be worn on the major festivals, the drabbest on penitential occasions, and ordinary ones on normal days. However, even allowing for this variation, it is clear that in many places dark or black vestments were used at Candlemas, and the pope or the bishop walked barefoot.

Faced with such an anomaly, liturgists have tried the usual trick of explaining away something that baffles them by suggesting that it is a hangover from a pagan festival (the Roman *Lupercalia*). But clearly this sort of device does not work. Far more likely is it to see in these penitential traits a reflection of the ambiguity of the occasion, the Gospel for the day, and the bearing of candles in procession before dawn. A penitential procession was known for a short time in Constantinople, but it clearly died out, so that this feature (so far as we know) is only known in the West. But that does not disqualify the authenticity of the custom. Purple vestments for the procession leading into white vestments for the Mass were the standard use of the Roman Catholic Church until the 1970 Missal, just as they were for the Easter Vigil. Nowadays, there is a temptation to make liturgy systematic and logical, so that anomalies and ambiguities have to go. Such an 'Enlightenment' attitude usually 'endarkens' liturgical experience, especially in the interests of 'relevance'.

At the Reformation, of course, the processions and all that preceded the Mass were abolished by Anglicans and Lutherans, though the feast was kept. As with Christmas and Epiphany, 1662 added its own explication, this time a happier one, for in addition to 'The Purification of St Mary the Virgin' there came 'The Presentation of Christ in the Temple'. Furthermore, Anna, who has not figured in the medieval English gospel-lections for this day, was restored.

Twentieth-century revisions have produced little that is startlingly new. The 1970 Missal simplifies the old rite, so that the candle-blessings are reduced from five to one (two texts are available). This has the advantage of clarity, but also cuts down on the possible repertoire of themes within the prayers themselves. The Preface is new, as is also that contained in our new service book. The Post-Communion is taken from the 1738 Paris Missal; this forms the basis of ours, too, except that Anna is included in addition to Simeon.

Other Anglican service books have not so far made a great deal of this feast, although there are some texts in the American Episcopal Book of Occasional Services (1979). In providing services for this day, care has been taken to allow for different circumstances and traditions. First of all, there is a Vigil-based service, which can lead straight into the Eucharist. It starts in the usual way with the *Lucernare,* and goes on through a rich series of Old Testament lections which serve to illuminate all the main features of the gospel narrative. Most of the chants between these readings are adapted from various hymns of the Byzantine offices for this day.

Secondly, there is a form for the Eucharist. We have already discussed the sources for this material. Because of the many possibilities for exegesis and reflection on the Gospel, the chance has been taken to provide a three-year scheme, in which the Gospel is the same throughout. Year 'A' is strong on judgement, 'B' on priesthood', and 'C' on incarnation. Thirdly, however, there is the question of the procession. In the Roman rite, the practice has been – and still is – to precede the Eucharist with a procession, although this is often a somewhat attenuated affair. Carpeted churches may wish to be restrained! But the procession is so much part of the day that it is a pity to leave it out altogether. John Baldovin has recently written a fascinating account of the 'stational' (i.e. processional) liturgies of Jerusalem, Rome and Constantinople, and has brought out many hidden insights into the way in which urban Christians took their environment so seriously.

At Candlemas, as well as on other occasions in the Christmas cycle, the Church has the opportunity to process, and the possibilities are going to vary. In some situations, it is only going to be possible to hold a procession inside the church building. In others, an outdoor procession may well be appropriate, particularly if this festival is observed on a Sunday and there is a large congregation. We who tend to scorn cities and prefer the romanticism of the countryside forget that the Bible begins in a garden but ends in a city. Baldovin has this to say about some of the greatest treasures in the liturgical tradition of the Church: 'It was by means of the attractiveness of the city as a sacred place that some of the major formulations of Christian worship were able to spread throughout Christendom.' In the services there are options as to where the procession takes place. The era of evening Masses finds in this feast a natural, if atmospheric home. In addition to the traditional pre-Mass procession, it is also suggested that the main service should *end* with a procession. This is because it has become apparent that this festival, if it is to live its own life to the full, is not only the end of the Christmas cycle but the pre-beginning of the Easter cycle. As a thoroughly biblical feast, based on a unique biblical narrative, it not only looks back to the incarnation but forward to the atonement, and since one of the purposes of the new services is to explore how best to link these doctrinal axes together, to end the main liturgy of this day with a procession that actually extinguishes the candles and has Ash Wednesday, Lent, Holy Week and Easter in prospect is a highly appropriate innovation and one that truly carries the spirit of the festival into the body of the liturgy. It is also possible to centre the procession round the solemn reading of the Gospel, a further illumination of the feast.

But whatever is done and however it may be done, it is crucial on this particular occasion to see not a piece of church fluff in the breeze but rather a whole dynamic of relationships, covering all ages and interests, in which the wider 'family' of the Church, brought together not by inheritance but by faith, celebrates together the paradoxical and bittersweet love of God for all people.

II

One of the surprises for many who pick up for the first time *The Promise of His Glory* or this commentary will be the crucial place it gives to 2 February, the Presentation of Christ in the Temple. For a long time it has been ignored by most, and misunderstood by more. It has been a day for the High Church, and has concentrated on purification to the exclusion of other themes, and then has seen purification only in terms of the Virgin Mary, making the feast one of her alone. *The Promise of His Glory* seeks to rescue it and to give it that pivotal place in the Christian year, looking back to Christmas at the end of an incarnation season and forward to Lent and a season of the passion. All through the book there have been hints that this is where it is leading. The introduction to this chapter in *The Promise* spells it out forcefully, and Kenneth Stevenson has already shown how the bitter-sweet nature of the day is there in the gospel story and has been celebrated in the liturgy through many centuries, and needs now to be recovered.

It needs to be recovered, not so much because it gives us a longer incarnation season, though that is gain, nor because it rounds off that season rather neatly (indeed in this book we have been wary of liturgy that is too neat and has everything conveniently compartmentalized and packaged), but because the gospel truths that the Presentation highlights are crucial, and supremely because a day that relates so directly the birth of the Lord to his death brings out something quite vital that is usually lost. The Collect of the Annunciation, another of those feasts of our Lord so often hijacked for our Lady, prays

> that as we have known the incarnation of your Son Jesus Christ
> by the message of an angel,
> so by his cross and passion
> we may be brought to the glory of his resurrection.

But it is the Presentation, rather than the Annunciation, that brings those two together and shows their relationship. The Annunciation links them only because of where it comes in the calendar. The Presentation has it there in its story.

This shift from birth to death, from incarnation to passion, is expressed most strongly in the ending of the Candlemas Liturgy, and this is discussed below. But the ambivalence of the day should not be expressed only through one liturgical movement and text; it should permeate the whole day. The lectionary helps to do this, and various texts in the services ensure that the passion element is not lost; but still much depends on sensitive handling locally. The lectionary allows one of the themes to become a little more dominant once in three years, but it should be only a *little* more. The Presentation must not be tidied up with one clear theme. Its power lies in its undercurrents.

The choice of music and hymnody must be faithful to this. To give an example, *one* hymn in honour of the Virgin ensures that the purification of Mary is not lost. *Four* hymns in her honour exclude other themes just as crucial. One hymn that needs to be added to the repertoire of many churches is John Ellerton's 'Hail to the Lord who comes' (AMNS 314, NEH 157), with its fine sixteenth-century tune, the 'Old 120th' – it holds together so much of what this day celebrates:

Hail to the great First-born
Whose ransom-price they pay!
The Son before all worlds,
The Child of man today,
That he might ransom us
Who still in bondage lay.

O Light of all the earth,
Thy children wait for thee!
Come to thy temples here,
That we, from sin set free,
Before thy Father's face
May all presented be!

A word needs to be said about the gospel canticle of Candlemas, *Nunc Dimittis*. Naturally it has an important place in the liturgy of the day, not only as part of the gospel story, but also as sung in procession. *The Promise of His Glory* provides the traditional Prayer Book text, for this is still the one to which the majority of people relate. For those wanting a modern translation, it has preferred the new ELLC text to that in the ASB, and this does show some improvement in what remains a difficult text to render in good modern English. Something is, of course, lost when psalms and canticles are turned into hymns, but, in communities where a sung *Nunc Dimittis* seems an impossibility, there are at least two satisfactory metrical versions. The better known is Bishop Dudley-Smith's 'Faithful vigil ended' (AMNS 453, NEH 44, HTC 55), which can be sung to the well-known tune, 'Pastor pastorum'. Unfortunately this version, which is otherwise admirable, relies heavily on the New English Bible's ugly 'Thou givest his discharge in peace' (from which the Revised English Bible mercifully releases us). The other is Michael Perry's 'Jesus, hope of every nation' (HTC 58), which is less of a direct translation, but reflects the feel of the day effectively.

So much for the character of the day. But when is it to be celebrated? In the last chapter, in relation to the Epiphany, the pros and cons of moving festivals like these to a Sunday were discussed. *The Promise of His Glory* comes down in favour of Sunday observance of the Presentation, in order that this turning point in the Christian cycle should be shared by all. In some churches this will open up the possibility of two Candlemas services, and we are given two in the book, a Vigil Service and the Candlemas Eucharist.

The Vigil Service is in the style of those provided earlier in the book – a Service of Light, with a series of readings, canticles and responsories. But this one has a higher profile and, unlike the provision for All Saints, Advent, Christmas and Epiphany, a full text is given, whereas the others rely on local initiative to devise from the resources given. This one is given a special place because here the light theme belongs not only to the opening *Lucernare*, but is carried forward through the various sections, and especially in the collects, to the procession and the *Nunc Dimittis* at the climax. There are other special features. Mention has already been made of the chants after the readings which are drawn from the Byzantine rite, full of rich imagery and teaching. There is an Intercession Prayer and a form of Concluding Prayer different from that given for the Eucharist.

When and how should this rite be used? Like all the vigil services, it can be used the night before the festival, as a preparation for it, whether in a great gathering, or quite simply by a small group. When used in that way, as a preparation for a celebration next day, any procession needs to be preliminary and to lead *to* the place where that main celebration will take place – from nave to sanctuary, for instance. It would be wrong to have the feeling that the festival season was over before the Candlemas Eucharist had been celebrated.

The possibility of a Sunday observance of the Presentation will, however, make it more likely that this service will be an evening service on the festival day after a morning Eucharist. This would be a good use of it. But, again, the nature of the procession needs to be thought through carefully. Candlemas can only sustain one final procession away from the altar with words that say, in effect, 'Christmas is over; turn to Lent'. In some communities, that procession and the texts that go with it may need to be lifted from the Eucharist and added to this vigil service, so that that ending becomes the pivotal change from birth to passion. In other communities, that procession and important mood shift will have taken place at the morning Eucharist, when more people will have been present to experience it. In that case, this evening rite needs to be the first service to take on the new penitential mood, and it has the potential to be that.

In short, here is a fine service, for use in full or as a resource, but its use needs to be thought through creatively and sensitively in relation to the Eucharist, to which we now turn.

The president's introduction to the day's liturgy after the opening greeting sets the tone, and seeks to ensure that the whole service, and not just the gospel reading or the procession, carries the message of the sword that will pierce.

> As a sign of his coming among us, his mother was purified, as we now come to him for cleansing . . .
>
> In this eucharist, we celebrate both the joy of his coming and his searching judgement, looking back to the day of his birth and forward to the coming days of his passion.

There are three main areas that need to be thought through in this service: the place of the procession, the use of candles, and the way the service ends. All three are of course related.

Two forms of the service have been provided. The mainstream text assumes a procession at the end; a second version retains it, where the Roman rite does, at the beginning. For those used to a Candlemas procession at the beginning (and most churches, of course, are not used to one, at the beginning, or in the middle, or at the end!), the preferred position at the end will seem strange. Yet it has always seemed a little odd to approach the altar singing 'Lord, now lettest thou thy servant depart in peace'! The move to the end is probably one of the most creative things in the whole book. It is not just another of those pieces of tidying up that takes half the fun out of worship, but has a strong theological purpose, all the stronger when the procession can end, as in many churches, at or near the font. The closing Responsory, which serves for Post-Communion Prayer,

> Here we have offered the Church's sacrifice of praise.
> **Help us, who have received the bread of life,**
> **to be thankful for your gift**

and later for Blessing and Dismissal,

> Here we bless one another in your name.
> **Help us, who now go in peace,**
> **to shine with your light in the world,**

also spells out in simple gesture the transition from Christmas to Easter. The congregation has processed, with lighted candles, from the altar to the font, and there they say,

> Here we have greeted the Light of the World.
> **Help us, who now extinguish these candles,**
> **never to forsake the light of Christ.**

Then they blow out their candles, but that isn't the end (what an anticlimax it would be!), for they continue, as they stand by the font,

> Hear we now stand near the place of baptism.
> **Help us, who are marked with the cross,**
> **to share the Lord's death and resurrection.**
>
> Here we turn from Christ's birth to his passion.
> **Help us, for whom Lent is near,**
> **to enter deeply into the Easter mystery.**

That transition cannot be made so powerfully when the procession has come at an earlier point, and churches with another tradition would do well to look again to see whether a concluding procession would not serve the day better. Nevertheless, where other arguments prevail – and there are churches where the font is in the wrong place or the architecture cries out for a procession movement the other way – *The Promise* does provide the alternative way of doing things, with the procession at the beginning.

A variation on it is the procession at the Gospel. In places where there is much space, and the possibility of the whole of the first part of the rite in a separate place or separate part of the church, the procession with candles after the reading of the gospel story can make a lot of sense. Here Nunc Dimittis is used at a natural place, just when it has been read in the Gospel. But Anna must not (as in the ASB) be omitted – and not just because of the desire to 'make women visible' in the liturgy!

Whenever the procession takes place it is, as always, desirable, that everybody be participant, not spectator, however untidy and cramped it all may be. Watching other people process is not the same, and pilgrimages are not spectator sports! But if it is absolutely impossible for all to move (and there is outside the building as well as inside to consider), then at least let all turn to the new focus. 'Here we *face* the place of baptism . . .'

There are questions to consider relating to the candles. How long should they be alight? This is difficult, for the ideal at a 'candle Mass' must surely be throughout? Yet, there are practical problems. Through a sermon, if it is more than a short homily, may be difficult, and through the distribution of communion very tricky. If the procession is to be at the end and candles are not lit until then, there is no problem, but it seems a pity not to have them alight during the gospel reading with its proclamation of 'the light to enlighten the nations'. But if they are lit twice, when is the Blessing Prayer to be said, and what happens when they are extinguished? The Blessing Prayer in *The Promise* is particularly fine:

> Lord God, springing source of everlasting light,
> pour into the hearts of your faithful people
> the brilliance of your eternal splendour,
> that we, who by these kindling flames
> light up this temple to your glory,
> may have the darkness of our souls dispelled,

> and so may be counted worthy to stand before you
> in that eternal temple where you live and reign . . .

It might be sufficient to use this prayer immediately before the procession, even when candles have been alight at an earlier point, such as the Gospel, and this is what *The Promise* implies. An earlier lighting does not preclude the prayer coming just before the procession.

The putting out of candles is always a difficult moment. Reference was made in the last chapter to the unfortunate symbolism in baptism when the light of Christ is extinguished as soon as it is given! There is often a sense of anticlimax when the instruction is given to blow the candles out. The Final Responsory above deals with it imaginatively to change the mood. At earlier points in the service (if, for instance, candles are to be extinguished after the Gospel and before the Sermon) it is better to blow them out on a 'high' and this probably means a strong acclamation with candles held high, than to have it happen rather surreptitiously and apologetically. Better the preacher or the choir pick up on the Gospel with the Acclamation given at this point:

> Today the Lord is presented in the temple in substance of our mortal nature.
> **Alleluia!**
> Today the Blessed Virgin comes to be purified in accordance with the law.
> **Alleluia!**
> Today old Simeon proclaims Christ as the Light of the nations and the glory of Israel.
> **Alleluia! Praise to Christ, the light of the world**.

Out go the candles on a 'high'!

All that remains after the Candlemas Liturgy is over is to ensure that the change of mood that has been proclaimed is maintained. There can be no question of ending Candlemas in the way suggested and then coming back to keep another Sunday of Epiphany. After the Presentation, the crib goes away, the best altar hangings and vestments disappear until Easter, and we move into 'ordinary time' until Ash Wednesday. In some years this will be just a few days, in others a month. Its Sundays will need to be designated 'Sundays before Lent' or 'before Easter'. Even if the Prayer Book and the ASB are still keeping Sundays after Epiphany, with this approach to the Christian cycle the change needs to be made at Candlemas.

The liturgical colour will change from white. Where churches have a sequence of just four colours, and purple is for Lent, then it will be a change into green for a while. Where churches have other varieties – a blue, for instance – this would be appropriate with a further change on Ash Wednesday.

As far as the lectionary is concerned, these Sundays before Lent can continue to use ASB and BCP provision – the collects and readings in those books are not unsuitable, only the name of the Sunday, and the use of the Epiphany Preface, Blessing, etc. Or this may be the chance to use some of the provisions in Lectionary B (see next chapter). The mood, whether the season is short or long depending on the date of Easter, is a 'limbering up for Lent', in much the way that an older generation understood the three mysteriously named Septuagesima, Sexagesima and Quinquagesima Sundays.

EIGHT

Lectionary

I

> Blessed Lord, who has caused all Holy Scriptures
> to be written for our learning:
> Grant that we may in such wise hear them,
> read, mark, learn, and inwardly digest them,
> that by patience and comfort of thy holy word,
> we may embrace and ever hold fast the blessed hope
> of everlasting life, which thou hast given us
> in our Saviour Jesus Christ.

When Thomas Cranmer set about writing collects for the 1549 Prayer Book, he tended to translate, and occasionally embroider upon the corresponding collect in the Sarum Missal, but on twenty-four occasions he went his own way, and the Second Sunday in Advent was one of them. Of these two dozen occasions, he composed collects four times on the Gospel for the day, and no fewer than eight on the Epistle. This was one of them, for it is the well-known passage about the purpose of Scripture (Romans 15.4ff.). We can only hazard a guess at why he did it. Perhaps he found the old Latin collect for the day a bit colourless. Perhaps he wanted to take the opportunity of writing something entirely of his own. No one will ever know.

But we all know the result, and it is not clear if that result would have been entirely to Cranmer's liking. Advent 2 has survived into the ASB lectionary in some disguise, but not sufficient to prevent many people calling this 'Bible Sunday'. In my youth, I frequently heard sermons that were little to do with the Bible, except if I was on a family holiday in Denmark, but then I was not able to understand much of what was being said. In the past thirty years or so, there has been quite a revolution in the way clergy of all traditions approach the question of preaching. A lot of the old liberal moralism has gone, and preachers pay far more heed to the gospel lection, so that congregations come to expect a biblically based sermon. The net result is that the old 'Bible Sunday' sticks out more and more like a sore thumb, rather like those 'children's corners' that used to appear in churches. If we are a family, then the *whole* church is the children's corner. If we are a people of the book, then *every* Sunday is Bible Sunday.

And that brings us to look again at how we use the Bible in worship, in particular at the lectionary. As is well known, the Prayer Book adapted the mass-reading scheme that appeared in the Sarum Missal; and the Lutherans on the Continent did much the same with their Latin Missals. There was a conservative editorial job done by both Churches and the result was that for four hundred years after the Reformation, Roman Catholics, Anglicans and Lutherans were using roughly the same scheme. Lutherans added their extra 'preaching texts', and, in some places, added a second year, basing many of their choices around the existing one-year set. Ironically however, in the very century in which ecumenism was born, that commonality of lectionaries has disappeared – for very good reasons and with the best of intentions.

In this country, the (ecumenical) Joint Liturgical Group produced a pattern for Sunday lections based on a two-year cycle, with a semi-thematic approach (some would say entirely thematic, but that is not what the compilers say!). This was published in 1967, and, with adaptations, was incorporated into the service books of the British Methodists (1975), the Church of Scotland (1979), and the United Reformed Church (1980), as well as the ASB (1980). Beginning with the most major change of all, it started with nine Sundays before Christmas, beginning with Creation and Fall, and went through the main Christmas and Easter cycles in an innovative manner, and numbered the ferial season 'after Pentecost', a happy restoration of a practice more traditional than the late medieval 'after Trinity'.

Meanwhile, the Roman Catholic Church underwent the Vatican II experience and decided to make the Scriptures more accessible to everyone, first by reading them in the vernacular, and then by deciding to produce an entirely new lection scheme. It was first used officially from Advent 1969. Based on a three-year series, it set out to bring the insights of biblical scholarship to bear on the way passages were selected.

In discussing the readings for some of the special occasions in the Christmas cycle, we have already encountered some of these questions in a tangential manner within these pages. If the British JLG scheme is the result of the 'biblical theology' movement, the Roman Catholic series can be said to stem partially at least from the 'redaction-criticism' school, whereby individual authors of biblical books are allowed, within the confines of reading set passages at public worship, to speak for themselves. This is most apparent when it comes to the Gospels themselves. Year 'A' concentrates on Matthew's Gospel, year 'B' on Mark, and year 'C' on Luke. Because Mark is shorter than the other two, John takes over when there is room, and John has traditional prominence as the 'spiritual Gospel' (as Clement of Alexandria puts it) on the major occasions. As far as is possible, the epistle readings try to read through the various books, although this has not proved practicable, for obvious reasons, with the Old Testament. The reading of the Old Testament at the Eucharist has proved the single most ecumenical restoration of this century. For the first time since the early centuries, this part of the Bible has been exposed to eucharistic congregations in a regular pattern, although the Armenian and Milanese rites never through the centuries lost the Old Testament at Mass.

The Promise of His Glory has adapted this three-year scheme so that the season pre-Advent to Candlemas has some coherence and can be used on its own without undue difficulty. It starts, as we have already seen, three Sundays before Advent (the three Sundays of the Kingdom), but the two Sundays immediately preceding may be kept as the Sunday of All Saints' Day (thus observing the Octave) and making the festival available to a larger congregation than might be possible), and the Dedication Festival, which in practice will make it near the end of October, the very month at the beginning of which the English Church on the eve of the Reformation (in 1536) laid down that it should be observed everywhere. Many churches already keep a Dedication Festival around that time, so that the new provisions will not make a great deal of difference. The readings for the Sunday just before Advent, of course, reflect the festival of Christ the

King, which is an occasion instituted by Pius XI in 1925 for the end of October but which found a more comfortable place at the end of the Church Year in the 1969 scheme. It should be noted that care was taken to bring out the Kingship of Christ over the *whole universe* when the new Missal was produced, and the three-year lectionary enabled the riches of the Bible to be used to illustrate the Kingship of Christ in a fuller manner. Other festivals are to be found in the Lectionary, and these are divided into two groups, in an obvious order of importance. The Advent and Christmas scheme we have already looked at. This is an area where the ASB (following Joint Liturgical Group) is least happy and most incongruous, even given the problems of finding an exact chronology through the infancy narratives. The Sundays after Epiphany deal with the *early* ministry of Christ. This has been the traditional rationale, which the JLG lectionary altered, by its use of themes from Christ's ministry.

Against the background of all this lectionary activity, based as it is on sound biblical scholarship, the collect for the Second Sunday in Advent in its Prayer Book version can read a little like a straw in the wind. But the time is coming when we shall have to realize that *all* lectionaries are provisional, and while there would seem to be a variety among the Churches (and congregations within the same Church) that is nothing less than baffling, still we may well be moving towards a basic 'Common' lectionary that could result from further adaptation of the Roman Catholic three-year scheme. Such has been tried out among the mainline Protestant Churches of the USA, Australia and New Zealand, and elsewhere. One of the criticisms that is frequently made about the ASB is the fact that all those pages are wasted by printing all the biblical lessons in full *and* in different versions. The next step may be something different. But that is another story.

Meanwhile, the Lectionary in *The Promise of His Glory* is offered as an interim. It has a unity about it and it mops up much of the mess that the ASB readings make. No one lectionary is completely consistent, nor perfect. But this one may well open up whole new vistas to preachers and congregations alike, and enable them to 'read, mark, learn and inwardly digest' God's word for today.

II

Because the lectionary in *The Promise of His Glory* is interim and provisional, those who plan worship have to be able to find their way into it from the usual BCP or ASB lectionaries, and then back out again at the end. What we have in the Church of England now is a new three-year lectionary, not far removed from the Roman one that has met such widespread ecumenical approval (not the first time in Anglicanism, for the Scottish Prayer Book had a three-year lectionary for Sunday Morning and Evening Prayer, calling the years A, B and C, as far back as 1929!), but only from All Saints' Day to Candlemas and again for a week before and after Easter. There are Churches that use the three-year lectionary for other parts of the year, and there is pressure to authorize this. But those who want to remain within the legal provision will find the way to transfer to *The Promise* lectionary set out in Chapter 2 of this book and how to get back to the BCP or ASB after Candlemas as set out in Chapter 7.

There are, in fact, two lectionaries in *The Promise of His Glory*, though both coincide for the period from Advent 3 until Epiphany 2. During this period nothing should deflect Christian congregations from hearing of John the Baptist, the Annunciation, the Birth of Jesus, the Coming of the Wise Men and the Baptism of the Lord, with the other incarnational material that is woven into that period of three or four weeks.

Outside that period there is more freedom. What is emerging is the concept of 'open' and 'closed' seasons in the Christian year. In the open seasons, where there are not overwhelming and compelling themes that dominate, churches should be free to select lectionary material that seems appropriate to them. This will vary from year to year, will take into account where that community is in terms of its discipleship, and will be part of a systematic teaching and preaching programme. The most obvious open seasons are between Pentecost Sunday and All Saints' Day and between Candlemas and Ash Wednesday.

In the closed seasons, the Christian Church needs to come together to celebrate and reflect upon the central mysteries of the faith. Here it becomes much more important that we be in step, and the lectionary contributes to that in a considerable way. Without a fairly strict demarcation of these seasons and an adherence to them, the whole liturgical cycle collapses. In these closed seasons local selection of lectionary material should give way to something the whole Church shares. The most obvious closed seasons are between Advent 3 and Epiphany and between Palm Sunday and Pentecost.

But the logic of *The Promise of His Glory* is that the Christmas closed season runs for far longer – beginning back on All Saints' Day and ending on the Presentation – and all the arguments for that have been well rehearsed both throughout *The Promise* and in this commentary. The whole eschatological thrust of the November material and incarnational emphasis of the January material, and the whole coherence of the season from All Saints to Candlemas, points to this. Lectionary 1 proceeds on that assumption.

Lectionary 2 allows greater flexibility and a more generous view of what constitutes an open season. For use at any time, outside the Advent 3 to Epiphany 2 period, it provides a whole series of helpful biblical units, of different duration (four to five weeks is average), that will allow a church community to explore new areas and widen its teaching and preaching approach. Many of the themes accord well with the general flavour of the pre- and post-Christmas seasons; others are more neutral, and would be appropriate at any point in the year. Those who are most attracted to Lectionary 1's long closed season will nevertheless find good material in Lectionary 2 for the post-Candlemas period and for other parts of the year.

Lectionary 1, in addition to providing generously for the Sundays and principal festivals of the period from All Saints to Candlemas also gives better provision than in the past for others saints' days. As well as the more familiar ones like St Andrew, the Conversion of St Paul and the Christmas saints, we have St Nicholas and the Conception of the Blessed Virgin Mary, for instance. As with *Lent, Holy Week, Easter,* where there was a plea that saints' days should not cut across the particular character of a season unnecessarily, so here in the period of the year we are now dealing with, the same applies. With many of the saints in the calendar at this time of the year, it may be sufficient, even in a church with daily services, simply to commemorate the saint in the Prayers of Intercession, and not to lose too often the flavour of the season. If you celebrate Advent Sunday and then go into a string of white festival days for Nicholas Ferrar, Francis Xavier, Ambrose of Milan and the blessed Santa Claus himself, Advent is in danger of evaporation! Let the season set the tone.

Nevertheless certain of these days, far from cutting across the distinctive character of the season, can enhance it. Just as St Stephen, St John and the Holy Innocents, sensitively used, and with the fine propers now provided, do not destroy the Christmas emphasis, but add a new dimension to it, so a careful use of *some* of the saints' days at other points can enhance it. For instance, both St Nicholas and the Conception of Mary can be brought into the feel of the Advent build-up, and not cut across it, and the lectionary provision sets out to help hold feast and season together.

The Lectionary chapter of *The Promise of His Glory* indicates something about the use of collects, and another chapter sets out a marvellous resource of them. For each day for which readings are provided a suggested collect is given. For some days, where the lectionary provision has a different emphasis in each of the three years, different collects are suggested for each year. This raises questions for those used to the BCP and ASB approach to collects.

The BCP provides a collect for each week, not over-thematic in tone, except on certain feast days where the theme is inescapable, and those who have followed that tradition expect the collect to be unchanging whatever the service and whatever the day, right through the week, except for an occasional change for a saint's day.

The ASB has gone a long way down the thematic path and

appears to believe that the collect is a kind of opening prayer for the Ministry of the Word. Thus, for instance, on the Seventh Sunday before Christmas, when the Sunday eucharistic lections are about Abraham, so is the collect about Abraham. This has had strange consequences when the collect for the whole week picks up on this Abraham theme even at services where the lectionary provides nothing about Abraham at all.

The Promise takes a different line, but is closer to the Prayer Book approach. An unchanging collect throughout the week, or for a particular Sunday year in year out, is not thought particularly important. The collect at any service should not be narrowly thematic, least of all spell out explicitly a theme that is not to be developed, but it should reflect the feel and character of the day, and so have a kind of seasonal appropriateness. Help is provided in finding the right collect, but in the end it is more a sense of asking what would be helpful than what is ordered. Certainly the superimposing of the ASB collects on the lectionaries of *The Promise* would, at points, be a nonsense. This would be less so with the BCP, but at certain crucial points between Advent 2 and Epiphany 2 would be almost as disastrous. The collect must be a prayer appropriate to the character of the day and one that draws the people into prayer at the beginning of the liturgy or, better still, draws together a time of silent prayer that precedes it.

The lectionary provision in *The Promise of His Glory*, and, indeed, the whole book with its rich provision of biblical canticles and responsories, broadens our use of Scripture, and especially widens our view of what it is that this season from 1 November to 2 February is all about. Nine familiar lessons enveloped in carols is no substitute for this treasury of Scripture from All Saints' Day to Candlemas.

Select Bibliography

Liturgical Year

(general studies which deal with Advent-Candlemas)

Adolf Adam, *The Liturgical Year*. New York: Pueblo, 1981.

Thomas J. Talley, *The Origins of the Liturgical Year*. New York: Pueblo, 1986.

Biblical Background

Raymond Brown, *The Birth of the Messiah*. New York: Doubleday, 1977.

Raymond Brown, *A Coming Christ in Advent*. Collegeville, MN: Liturgical Press, 1988.

Raymond Brown, *An Adult Christ at Christmas*. Collegeville, MN: Liturgical Press, 1977.

Raymond Brown, articles in *Worship* (including some of the material in the two foregoing books).

The Season of Advent to Candlemas

J. D. Crichton, *The Coming of the Lord: Advent to Candlemas, Origins of the Feasts and Seasons with Homily Notes*. Rattleden: Kevin Mayhew, 1990.

Eltin Griffin, ed., *Celebrating the Season of Advent*. Leominster: Fowler Wright, 1987.

Individual Studies

B. D. Spinks, 'Revising the Advent-Christmas-Epiphany Cycle in the Church of England'. *Studia Liturgica* 17 (1987), pp. 176–90.

Kenneth W. Stevenson, 'The Origins and Development of Candlemas: A Struggle for Identity and Coherence?', *Ephemerides Liturgicae* 102 (1988), pp. 316–46 (also in J. Neil Alexander, ed., *Time and Community: In Honor of Thomas Julian Talley* (Washington: Pastoral Press, 1990), pp. 43–76.)

John Wilkinson, *Egeria's Travels to the Holy Land*. London: SPCK, 1971; Warminster: Aris and Phillips, 1981.